WATERLOO

By the same author

The Holy Fox: A Life of Lord Halifax
Eminent Churchillians
The Aachen Memorandum
Salisbury: Victorian Titan
Napoleon and Wellington
Hitler and Churchill: Secrets of Leadership
(ed.) *What Might Have Been*

WATERLOO

June 18, 1815:
The Battle for Modern Europe

ANDREW ROBERTS

MAKING HISTORY
Series Editors: Amanda Foreman and Lisa Jardine

HarperCollins*Publishers*

HarperCollins books may be purchased for educational, business, or sales promotional use. For information, please write: Special Markets Department, HarperCollins Publishers Inc., 10 East 53rd Street, New York, NY 10022.

Published in Great Britain in 2005 by HarperCollins Publishers.

FIRST EDITION

Printed on acid-free paper

Library of Congress Cataloging-in-Publication Data is available upon request.

ISBN 0-06-008866-4

05 06 07 08 09   RRD   10 9 8 7 6 5 4 3 2 1

CONTENTS

ILLUSTRATIONS

General Hans von Zieten.

Marquis Emmanuel de Grouchy. *(Peter Newark's Military Pictures)*

General Pierre Cambronne declining to surrender. *(The Art Archive/Musée Thomas Dobrée, Nantes/Dagli Orti)*

Closing the Gates at Hougoumont, by Robert Gibb. *(© Trustees of the National Museums of Scotland)*

Wellington's handwritten orders to the commander inside Hougoumont. *(Private Collection/Bridgeman Art Library/Topfoto)*

Sergeant Charles Ewart captures the eagle standard of the French 45th Regiment. *(Peter Newark's Military Pictures)*

The Sunken Lane, by Lionel Edwards. *(The Mansell Collection/ Getty Images)*.

Marshal Ney Rallying the Troops at Waterloo, by Eugène Chaperon. *(Private Collection/Bridgeman Art Library)*

The Earl of Uxbridge directing sweeping-up cavalry operations towards the end of the battle.

Wellington meets Blücher after the battle. *(Engraving from the picture in the Palace of Westminster; by Lumb Stocks, after D. Maclise; published by The Art Union of London, 1875; India proof. V&A Images)*

The aftermath of Waterloo. *(Anne S.K. Brown Military Collection, Brown University Library)*

FOREWORD

The Duke of Wellington described the English victory at the battle of Waterloo as 'a damned nice thing – the nearest run thing you ever saw in your life'. As Andrew Roberts makes vividly clear in this gripping new account of the action leading up to and during the fateful battle of 18 June 1815, throughout that day the military advantage swung vertiginously towards and then away from Wellington's forces as the battle raged. The loss of life on both sides was devastating – this was a battle in which in some senses both sides could be termed the losers. In the end, though, the victory and the lasting glory deservedly fell to Wellington.

The outcome of the battle marked a crucial and lasting juncture in European history. Napoleon Bonaparte's defeat at Waterloo was his final downfall and the end of his imperial dream. Wellington's victory marked the beginning of a new English imperial adventure.

The battle of Waterloo, then, was one of those milestones in history – a marker, a turning point, an epoch-making incident, a directional laser-beam of light from the past to the future – on which our understanding of the past depends. Andrew Roberts's sharply-focused and economical account highlights the extraordinary way in which events on the ground at key moments in history shape forever what follows.

Waterloo launches an exciting series of small books edited by Amanda Foreman and Lisa Jardine – 'Making History' – each of which covers a 'turning point' in history. Each book in the series will take a moment at which an event or events made a lasting impact on the unfolding course of history. Such moments are of dramatically different character: from the unexpected outcome of a battle to a landmark invention; from an accidental decision taken in the heat of the moment to a considered programme intended to change the world. Each volume of 'Making History' will be guaranteed to make the reader sit up and think about Europe's and America's relationship to their past, and about the key figures and incidents which moulded and formed its process.

Amanda Foreman
Lisa Jardine

ACKNOWLEDGEMENTS

I would like to take this opportunity to thank Ian Fletcher of Ian Fletcher Battlefield Tours, who in 2000 conducted me around no fewer than sixteen Peninsular War and Waterloo Campaign battlefields, including several of Wellington's masterpieces, and who has always been tremendously supportive of my Napoleonic Wars endeavours. Peter Hofschröer has introduced me to the revisionist accounts of Waterloo, and to the importance of the Siborne model, which can be seen in the National Army Museum, from where Andrew Uffindell and Julian Farrance have also been most supportive.

I should also like to thank Peter Chambers of Bangor, County Down, for his generosity in giving me Sir William Fraser's book *The Waterloo Ball*.

Colonel John Hughes-Wilson, with whom I take annual three-day tours to sites of Napoleonic and Wellingtonian interest in London, France and Waterloo, has introduced me to many of the aspects of the battle that one can perhaps only fully appreciate by walking the ground itself. John, president of the Guild of Battlefield Guides, used to live near the battlefield and has conducted ninety tours of it, so I could not have been in better hands. He also very generously read my manuscript for me, as did John Morewood, editor of the excellent *Waterloo Journal*, the magazine of the Association of Friends of the Waterloo Committee, an organisation that all enthusiasts should join. I would like to thank both Johns most warmly.

This book is dedicated to Robin Birley, in grateful recognition of sixteen years of friendship and generosity.

ANDREW ROBERTS
www.andrew-roberts.net
October 2004

INTRODUCTION

'AFTER THE PUBLICATION of so many accounts of the battle of 18 June, it may be fairly asked on what grounds I expect to awaken fresh interest in a subject so long before the public.' Those words were written by Sergeant-Major Edward Cotton of the 7th Hussars as long ago as 1849, in his preface to a guidebook to the battlefield entitled *A Voice from Waterloo*. True enough then, how much more true are they when applied to yet another book on the battle published a century and a half and over one hundred books later. The answer that Cotton gave then is the one I would also give today: that while there are still doubts, mysteries, debates and confusions about the battle – let alone tremendous national bias evident in its retelling – there is always scope for another account.

'Never was a battle so confusedly described as that of Waterloo,' wrote the Swiss historian (and Marshal Ney's chief of staff) General Henri Jomini, and that is partly because it was such a momentous engagement. The Duke of Wellington himself likened the description of a battle to that of a ball – perhaps he had in mind the Duchess of Richmond's famous one three days before Waterloo – where there is so much simultaneous movement of so many people across so large an area with so many different outcomes that to record it all from a single standpoint becomes nigh-impossible.

Yet what we can say for certain about the battle of Waterloo –

that it ended forever the greatest personal world-historical epic since that of Julius Cæsar – is easily enough to drive us on to want to discover more. The political career of Napoleon Bonaparte, that master of continental Europe whose life was nonetheless punctuated by the three islands on which he was born, was exiled and died, came to a shuddering and total halt on the evening of Sunday, 18 June 1815. The Grande Armée which he had led across the sands of Egypt, the meadows of Prussia, the plains of Iberia, the hamlets of Austria and the snows of Russia, was finally and completely routed on the slopes of Mont St Jean twelve miles south of Brussels.

Of course Waterloo did not spell the end of the entire Bonapartist epic – that did not take place until Napoleon's great-nephew the Prince Imperial was speared to death by Zulu assegais in 1879 – but it did condemn the Emperor Napoleon I to ignominious exile and a subsequent early death on the Atlantic rock of St Helena. It also finally brought to an end no fewer than twenty-three almost unbroken years of French Revolutionary and subsequently Napoleonic Wars, and ushered in a period of peace in Europe that was to last – with a few short if sharp exceptions – for a century, until those self-same Low Countries fields were churned up once more with the mud and blood consequent upon similar hegemonic European ambitions.

What Lord Byron disapprovingly called 'the crowning carnage, Waterloo', and Alfred, Lord Tennyson, with more reverence in his panegyric poem to Wellington, 'that world-earthquake, Waterloo!', brought the eighteenth century to a full stop, or rather to a final exclamation mark. Despite taking place one-seventh of the way into the calendar nineteenth century, Waterloo was nonetheless essentially an eighteenth-century phenomenon. Historians sometimes write of 'the long' eighteenth century, a period starting with the English revolution of 1688 and ending in 1815, and it is right to see Waterloo as the end of both a geopolitical and a military era.

Ghastly as the carnage at Waterloo undoubtedly was, thenceforth wars were to be fought with the infinitely more ghastly methods of trenches (the Crimea), barbed wire, railways and machine-guns (the American Civil War), directed starvation (the Franco-Prussian War), concentration camps (the Boer War), and mustard gas and aerial bombardment (the First World War).[1] By the time of the Great War, chivalry was effectively dead as an element of war-making.

By contrast with today, when an enemy head of state constitutes a legitimate military target, Wellington refused an artillery officer under his command permission to fire his battery at Napoleon. The gorgeously-coloured uniforms worn in the Napoleonic Wars were replaced, by the time of the Boer War, with khaki and subsequently camouflaged uniforms, as troops sought to blend in with the surrounding country rather than bedazzle their enemies. For all that Waterloo was, like all battles, essentially about bringing death and maiming to the enemy, there was also a tangible spirit of *élan, esprit, éclat* and – at least initially – aesthetic beauty to the scene.

There was also plenty of chivalry shown on both sides at Waterloo; witness the reaction of the British infantry during the great French cavalry attack when, according to Ensign Howell Rees Gronow of the 1st Foot Guards:

> Among the fallen we perceived the gallant colonel of the hussars lying under his horse, which had been killed. All of a sudden two riflemen of the Brunswickers left their battalion, and after taking from their helpless victim his purse, watch, and other articles of value, they deliberately

put the colonel's pistols to the poor fellow's head, and blew out his brains. 'Shame!' 'Shame!' was heard from our ranks, and a feeling of indignation ran through the whole line.[2]

Captain (later Lieutenant-Colonel) William Tomkinson of the 16th Light Dragoons similarly recorded the occasion when 'An officer of cuirassiers rode close to one of our squares with a detachment of men. He saw he had no chance of success, and by himself alone rode full gallop against the square, was shot and killed. Our men and officers regretted his fate.'[3]

The generation after Waterloo saw, in the title of the great work of the distinguished historian Paul Johnson, *The Birth of the Modern*, and in one sense the battle was the midwife to this great act of world-historical obstetrics. With Napoleonic ambitions no longer subjecting Europe to campaign after campaign, Mankind could finally look ahead to a period of peace and progress.

Yet Napoleon himself had also been, at least in the early days of his rule, a great force for social and political modernisation. His absolute power had of course corrupted his regime absolutely, but before that happened he had swept away much of the obscurantism and backwardness of many of Europe's *anciens régimes*. Tyrant that he undeniably became, responsible for the deaths of hundreds of thousands though he undoubtedly was, a standing obstacle to peace as he certainly turned into, nonetheless Napoleon was not all bad, and certainly nothing like the ideological totalitarian monsters who followed him.

The battle that brought the Napoleonic juggernaut to its final halt and shattering collapse is worthy of all the exhaustive study and minute analysis that has been devoted to it. As one of its earliest and most perceptive chroniclers, General Sir James

Shaw Kennedy (who had fought in the campaign), wrote in the peroration of his classic *Notes on the Battle of Waterloo*:

> There can be no doubt that, so long as history is read, the battle of Waterloo will be much and eagerly discussed; and that, so long as the art of war is studied, its great features, and most important details, will form subjects of anxious inquiry and consideration by military men.[4]

And not just by military men. The enduring fascination of Waterloo is not just its sheer size, or its historical results, or the fact that Napoleon and Wellington had never faced each other across a battlefield before and never would again, or the strategy and tactics employed, or the tales of valour, or the famous and colourful individuals and regiments involved, or even the fact that it was 'a close run thing'; it is the unique combination of all those factors, and of so many more besides.

THE CAMPAIGN

THE WATERLOO CAMPAIGN began in earnest at 3.30 a.m. on Monday, 12 June 1815 when the Emperor Napoleon, exhibiting none of the torpor and lack of decisiveness that his supporters later claimed afflicted him, left Paris after a farewell dinner with his family and was quickly driven north in his carriage, crossing the Belgian border with an army of 124,000 men a mere three days later. He had only been in France for three months, having landed at Fréjus near Antibes from his island exile on Elba on 1 March.

Napoleon had initially hoped to regain his throne from the legitimate Bourbon monarch of France, King Louis XVIII, without a war, but on 13 March the rest of the European powers, then in congress at Vienna, had denounced him as an outlaw and a 'disturber of world repose'. Once Louis had fled Paris on 18 March and Napoleon had entered the Tuileries Palace the following day, it was perfectly clear to all that the Emperor would have to defeat at least four nations' armies to survive in power. Nor was time on his side.

Napoleon's strategy was really dictated to him by the fact that although vast enemy armies were being despatched towards France, they could only arrive at its borders piecemeal and so could, he hoped, be defeated one by one, through his employing the superior generalship that had allowed him to win all but ten of the seventy-two battles he had fought in his career.

Although it is very difficult to be accurate as to exact troop strengths throughout this period, Napoleon had roughly 20,000 troops under Marshal Davout in Paris, 85,000 guarding France's frontiers, 10,000 putting down the royalist revolt in La Vendée in western France, and 123,000 in the Armée du Nord. To add to these 238,000 effectives, around 115,000 French troops were either on leave or absent without leave, 46,000 conscripts were in training at depots, and there were National Guard units garrisoning border fortresses who could have been called upon were Napoleon to be granted more of his most precious commodity of all: time.

To march north quickly, defeat either the Anglo-Allied armies under the Duke of Wellington or the Prussian army under Marshal Gebhard von Blücher, Prince of Wahlstadt, would have the immediate effect of re-establishing *la Gloire*. As one historian has summarised Napoleon's plans: 'His object was to defeat one or the other before they had time to concentrate and then, forcing both back on their divergent communications, to enter Brussels as a conqueror. Thereafter . . . the Belgian common people would rise against the Dutch, the war-weary French take heart and unite behind him, the Tory government in London fall, and his Austrian father-in-law [Emperor Francis II], deprived of British subsidies, sue for peace.'[1]

There were other factors that imparted a sense of urgency to Napoleon's actions, principally the knowledge that British regiments were on their way back from America, no fewer than 200,000 Russians were marching towards France along with 210,000 Austrians, and a Spanish/ Portuguese force of around 80,000 might also take the field in the south. Napoleon therefore formulated a bold plan, as one might have expected from a commander who, though he had tasted catastrophic defeat in Russia in 1812, terrible reverses in 1813, and the humiliation of abdication in 1814, nonetheless remained one of the most formidable strategists of world history.

Even though over 700,000 Allied soldiers were being mobilised to defeat him, only a fraction of these were guarding Brussels – roughly 116,000 under Blücher and 112,000 under Wellington – and the Emperor had crushed six enemy coalitions in the past. Furthermore Wellington needed to leave some of his troops garrisoning Brussels.

The logistical, supply and communications problems involved in coordinating the coalition's efforts would, Napoleon hoped, be exacerbated by certain political differences that had emerged between them in Vienna. Whatever the odds against him, he was certainly not about to give up the chance of ruling France again, and of one day handing on his throne to his beloved son Napoleon, the King of Rome.

France had been exhausted by almost continual warfare since 1792, and although she despised the Bourbons and failed to support them on Napoleon's return, only a quick victory would encourage the majority – and especially the middle classes impoverished by twenty-three years of war – to return to his standard. Accordingly he set the nation to work to prepare for the coming invasion. Parisian workshops had been busy throughout April, May and the first half of June turning out over 1,200 uniforms per day and manufacturing twelve million cartridges. Muskets were produced at the impressive rate of 12,000 a month, with another thousand a month being repaired and reconditioned.

By the time his Armée du Nord crossed the River Meuse and captured Charleroi on Thursday, 15 June, it was as fine and as well-equipped a force as Napoleon had commanded in years, indeed since the loss of the flower of French manhood in the endless pine forests and frozen winter wastes of European Russia three years earlier. Yet because several of his former marshals had refused to serve under him, many of the rank-and-file of his army were highly suspicious of their officers; talk of treason abounded. 'Never,' wrote one historian, 'did Napoleon have so formidable or so fragile a weapon in his hand.'

It was a very different story for the Anglo-Allied force that had been under the command of Arthur Wellesley, 1st Duke of Wellington, only since April 1815. Although Wellington had been in overall command of the Anglo-Spanish-Portuguese forces that had fought in the Iberian Peninsula between 1808 and 1814, the army he now led had relatively few veterans of those fierce and brilliantly-fought campaigns. For the most part the heroes of Talavera, Badajoz, Salamanca and Vittoria were stationed in the far-off United States, where they had been fighting under Wellington's brother-in-law, General Sir Edward Pakenham, against the American commander and future president Andrew Jackson. Although peace had come in January 1815, few had had time to make the long Atlantic crossing home.

'I have got an infamous army,' Wellington had privately complained only the month before Napoleon crossed the Meuse, 'very weak and ill-equipped, and a very inexperienced staff. In my opinion they are doing nothing in England . . .' It was true that reinforcements had been slow to arrive in the Low Countries, so that by the opening of the campaign only a little over one-third of Wellington's 112,000-strong force was made up of British soldiers, of whom some had never before seen a shot fired in anger.

Yet that does not tell the whole story; in all there were thirty-nine infantry battalions from the British army and the King's German Legion (KGL), a crack unit loyal to George III that was equal in professionalism to any British one. Furthermore there were twenty-nine cavalry regiments, including several of the best in the army. As the distinguished Waterloo chronicler Ian Fletcher has observed: 'It was a pale shadow of the old Peninsular army, but there were, nevertheless, some fine regiments present, and the British contingent was certainly not the inexperienced and raw army . . . that some historians would have us believe.'[2] To underline this one has only to name some of those famous regiments present, such as the 1st Foot Guards, Coldstream Guards and 3rd Foot Guards, as well as the 30th, 42nd, 73rd and 95th line regiments, the 1st and 2nd Light KGL, the 1st and 2nd Life Guards, Royal Horse Guards, 1st (Royal) Dragoons, 6th (Inniskilling) Dragoons, 16th and 23rd Light Dragoons, 7th, 10th, 15th and 18th Hussars, and both light dragoons and hussars from the KGL.[3]

Despite his private misgivings, Wellington was still confident that if he and the Prussians under Marshal Blücher could coalesce successfully, victory would be theirs. One day he came across the diarist Thomas Creevey in the park at Brussels, who quizzed him about his plans. 'By God,' Wellington said, 'I think Blücher and myself can do the thing.' 'Do you calculate upon any desertion in Buonaparte's army?' asked Creevey. 'Not upon a man,' the Duke replied, 'from the colonel to the private in a regiment – both inclusive. We may pick up a Marshal or two, perhaps, but not worth a damn.' Wellington then spotted a British private wandering in the park, looking up at the statues. 'There,' he said, pointing out the man to Creevey, 'it all depends on that article, whether we do the business or not. Give me enough of it, and I am sure.'[4]

The French army might have feared treachery in high places, but the Anglo-Allied high command was equally concerned about whether the Dutch and Belgian contingents, which made up a quarter of Wellington's force, would remain loyal in the field, not least those units which only the previous year had been in the service of the Emperor. Wellington's German troops – which made up another third of his force – ranged from the superb King's German Legion of 6,000 veterans to the less reliable contingents from Brunswick, Hanover and Nassau.

If Napoleon had cause not to fear the Anglo-Allied force overmuch, he could also feel relatively unperturbed about the 116,000 Prussians to his east. Although the numbers seemed large, over half the Prussian army was made up of *Landwehr* (militia) troops rather than regular soldiers, and many of them came from outside Prussia itself. Earlier in June a force of 14,000 well-equipped Saxons had mutinied and had to be removed from the theatre of operations. Yet the average Prussian regular soldier was a tough specimen, and no one in the army was tougher than the commander-in-chief, Prince Gebhard von Blücher, whose seventy-three years belied an offensive spirit second to none. His splendid nickname – *Marshal Vorwärts* ('Marshal Forwards') – was well-deserved.

Not everything about Blücher inspired confidence, however, since he suffered from occasional mental disturbances, including the delusions that he had been impregnated by an elephant and that the French had bribed his servants to heat the floors of his rooms so that he would burn his feet. The Prussian high command nonetheless exhibited a commendably broad-minded attitude towards these disorders; their army chief of staff General Gerhard von Scharnhorst wrote that Blücher 'must lead though he has a hundred elephants inside him'.

The only two coalition armies ready to fight Napoleon in June 1815 were Wellington's and Blücher's. The two commanders had met only twice in May, when they agreed on the broad outlines of a defensive strategy should they be attacked before the coalition had had time to deploy its huge forces. Wellington was deeply cognisant of the disastrous campaigns that the coalition had fought against Napoleon in front of Paris in 1814, when they had lost battle after battle through lack of coordination. 'I would not march a corporal's guard on such a system,' was his characteristically dismissive response to the failed strategy.

Napoleon's Orders for the Day were famous for their uplifting sentiments, and that of Thursday, 15 June was no different. He reminded his troops as they crossed into the Austrian Netherlands (roughly modern-day Belgium) that it was the anniversary of his great victories of Marengo in 1800 and Friedland in 1807. 'The moment has come,' he stated in his peroration, 'to conquer or to perish.'

Although British historians in the nineteenth century strove to conceal the fact, and Wellington himself denied it into old age, Napoleon's swift operation to take Charleroi on 15 June and to advance quickly towards Brussels took Wellington and to a lesser extent Blücher by surprise. There is still considerable (and surprisingly bitter) debate over exactly when Wellington heard the first truly reliable information about where Napoleon was and what he had done, and what the first Allied troop manoeuvres were in response, but Wellington's well-authenticated phrase 'Napoleon has humbugged me, by God! He has gained twenty-four hours' march on me!' has come down to us through history, and seems vividly to sum up his understandable reaction.[5]

Napoleon himself was worse than humbugged on 15 June when General Comte Louis Bourmont, one of his divisional commanders but nonetheless royalist in his politics, rode directly over to the Prussian 1st Corps commander General Hans von Zieten and surrendered to him with five of his staff. The information he was able to pass on about Napoleon's invasion plans was immediately vouchsafed to Marshal Blücher, who nonetheless seems to have failed to take proper advantage of it. There is even some doubt whether he passed on all the information to Wellington about Napoleon's proposed route to Brussels.[6] (This might well have been because Blücher suspected deliberate misinformation; he certainly felt that Bourmont's actions offended his sense of soldier's honour.)

At this point Napoleon split his forces, always a dangerous thing to do at the start of a major campaign. He ordered Marshal Michel Ney to march west to take the strategically important crossroads of Quatre Bras before Wellington could reinforce it. Quatre Bras stood at the junction of the Charleroi–Brussels and the Nivelles–Namur roads, and would thus give Napoleon extra leeway when it came to deciding how to make his approach on Brussels. Possession of the crossroads would have kept French strategic options open, and Ney was under no illusions about how much Napoleon wanted to capture it.

Meanwhile the Emperor marched off towards Ligny in the east in order to engage the Prussians, who he rightly estimated had come far too far south when Blücher had decided to invest Sombreffe. (Few of these place-names were towns in the modern sense, and some villages mentioned later, such as Plancenoit, were in 1815 little more than a collection of cottages and outhouses, but any stone walls at all could be invaluable in a musketry firefight.)

Napoleon did not write down his strategic plans, nor did he vouchsafe them to subordinates, and since virtually everything he would ever write about the Waterloo campaign was factually suspect and politically motivated, it is impossible to do more than surmise what he intended on 15 and 16 June. Yet one thing is near-certain: by risking splitting his forces he was hoping to be able to drive a wedge between the Anglo-Allied and the Prussian forces, and thereby deal with first one and then the other separately, in a microcosm of his overall plans for the division and destruction of all his enemies in the coalition.[7]

In this scheme Napoleon was enormously aided by the problems of communication during campaigns. Although semaphore and a very basic telegraph system were in existence in 1815, they were not comprehensive and did not extend across Belgium; neither were balloons in use on either side. Messages could thus only be sent at the speed of a galloping horse, and since there was much rain, and therefore mud, during the Waterloo campaign, this was consequently slower. The aides de camp who carried messages between commanders could be fired upon, captured, take wrong turnings, find that their quarries had moved on, or be subject to any number of problems that meant that messages – sometimes taken over significant distances – either never arrived or were delivered so late as to be utterly superseded by events. It was an occupational hazard of early-nineteenth-century warfare, and it seems to have struck particularly badly in the Waterloo campaign, on both sides.

Wellington might have complained about his inexperienced staff, but Napoleon too had to deal with a brand-new chief of staff, Marshal Soult, in the place of his long-standing and highly efficient Marshal Berthier, who had at first refused to take part in the campaign, and then had soon afterwards died in very mysterious circumstances, falling out of a high window on 1 June in Bamberg, Bavaria. Soult, a solidly professional soldier who had nonetheless been regularly defeated by Wellington during the Peninsular Wars, did not shine in his place.

On the night of 15 June, as Napoleon slept in Charleroi, Wellington and his senior officers were entertained at a great ball only thirty miles away in Brussels, at the invitation of the 4th Duke of

Richmond and Lennox and his wife. It was perhaps the most famous social occasion of the nineteenth century, and any criticisms that Wellington should have been paying attention to French troop movements rather than enjoying a party were waved away with the argument that it was important to show the citizens of Brussels that there was no need to panic. 'Duchess,' Wellington told his hostess, 'you may give your ball with the greatest safety, without fear of interruption.' By the time the ball in the rue de Blanchisserie had begun, however, Wellington had received definite news from the Prussians that Napoleon had indeed crossed the border.

A letter in the author's possession is worthy of quotation *in extenso* (see APPENDIX I), since it illustrates the lack of foreknowledge of many of those who attended the Duchess of Richmond's ball. Rumours were plentiful, not least when Wellington withdrew from the ballroom to confer with his most senior commanders in the Richmonds' study, but facts were thin. 'The lamps shone o'er fair women and brave men,' wrote Byron of that brilliant night, and as the ball began few could have suspected that only seventy-two hours later fully four in ten of the officers present would be either dead or wounded. (Although Byron mythologised the 'high hall' of the ballroom, in fact the occasion took place, according to the Richmonds' daughter Lady de Ros, 'in an old building that had once been a coachmaker's depot in which she and her sisters played in bad weather . . . A long, barn-like room; with small old-fashioned pillars.'[8])

For all that it was held in a coachmaker's barn, the evening was a glittering social occasion, the guests including the Prince of Orange (later King William II of Holland), the Duke of Brunswick (who fell the next day at Quatre Bras), the Prince of Nassau, the Earls of Conyngham, Uxbridge (commander of the British cavalry), Portarlington and March, as well as twenty-two colonels, sixteen *comtes* and *comtesses*, a large number of British peers and peeresses and a total of twenty-two people bearing the title of 'honourable', denoting the child of a peer. Whether it was a particularly romantic evening, however, must be doubted, since of the 224 people invited by the Richmonds there were only fifty-five women, of whom fewer than a dozen were unmarried.[9]

Wellington, who had assumed that Napoleon would advance on Brussels via Mons rather than taking the more direct Charleroi route, and who stuck to his assumption despite growing evidence to the contrary, was finally disabused during the ball by important and reliable information from the Prussians, who were expecting to fight at Sombreffe the next day, and from the commandant of the Mons garrison that there were no Frenchmen in sight. He had been 'humbugged' indeed, but he made up for it by trying to concentrate his army as quickly as possible upon Quatre Bras. 'This news was circulated directly,' recalled one of the guests, Lady Georgina Lennox, 'and while some of the officers hurried away, others remained at the ball, and actually had not time to change, but fought in evening costume.'[10]

The Duke of Richmond later told the tale that in his study Wellington had admitted that he would not be able to stop Napoleon at Quatre Bras, adding, 'And if so we must fight him here,' passing his thumbnail over the map and allowing Richmond to mark in pencil a village called Waterloo. To this author at least, the story sounds like a case of *esprit d'escalier*, a serviceable French phrase whose English translations smack too harshly of deliberate falsehood. Unfortunately the map that might have authenticated the tale was lost in Canada when Richmond was Governor-General there three years later.[11]

At 8 a.m. on Friday, 16 June Napoleon was informed that the

whole of the Prussian army seemed to have assembled at Sombreffe, so he left for the extreme right flank of his forces to check for himself, arriving at Fleurus at 11 a.m. Sure enough, the Prussians were there, so he ordered Marshal Ney, who he assumed would take the Quatre Bras crossroads with relative ease, to despatch a large body of his force to him to help rout the Prussians.

By the time Ney received Napoleon's rather florid instructions – 'The fate of France is in your hands. Thus do not hesitate even for a moment to carry out the manoeuvre' – he was no longer capable of carrying them out. For if Wellington had been relatively slow in concentrating his forces upon Quatre Bras, fearing that it might be a feint of Napoleon's, Ney had been still more dilatory, and by the time he started to try to take the crossroads the British reserve had already begun arriving there after a thirty-mile march. Although the credit for saving Quatre Bras must go to the initiative of General Constant Rebecque, the Dutch chief of staff, who was early on the scene and recognised its strategic importance, the actual outcome of the battle of Quatre Bras itself was due to Wellington himself.

Wellington had set out from Brussels at 3 a.m., and by 11 a.m. he was conferring with Blücher at the Brye windmill overlooking the battlefield of Ligny. It is said that he trained his telescope on Napoleon, the first time he had ever set eyes on the man with whose name his fame was to be forever inextricably linked. They had both been born on islands, they had both attended French military academies and spoke French as their second language; they were the same age, born within three months of one another in 1769; they both excelled at topography and chose Hannibal as their ultimate hero, yet they had never hitherto faced one another across a field of battle. Nor were they destined to on 16 June, since

Wellington only had time to give Blücher his considered opinion as to the Prussian displacements before being called off to command the defence of Quatre Bras.

The Duke politely criticised Blücher's decision to present the whole Prussian army to Napoleon's view – and artillery – in the old Continental manner, explaining his own preference of trying to conceal soldiers behind the reverse slopes of hills. 'My men prefer to see the enemy,' replied the proud, brave, but in this case also foolhardy Prussian. Wellington's private estimation as he rode off was: 'If they fight here, they will be damnably mauled.' Sure enough, when Napoleon attacked, they were.

Marshal Ney, the veteran of seventy battles, might have won the splendid soubriquet 'the bravest of the brave' in numerous engagements, but he was not an impressive commander when left in overall charge, and there were also fears that he had been suffering from a form of 'combat fatigue' or 'battle stress' ever since the gruelling Russian campaign of 1812, when he had been left to command the French rearguard after Napoleon had fled back to Paris. He had certainly become highly unpredictable by 1815, and was quite possibly simply burnt out as a soldier. Napoleon once complained that Ney understood less than the youngest drummer boy in the French army, and certainly piled complaint on complaint upon his actions – and inactions – during the Waterloo campaign when he was exiled on St Helena.

Ney, who had fallen for Wellington's tactic of concealing his troops in the Peninsular War, only attacked at Quatre Bras late and half-heartedly, even though Wellington was not on the battlefield in the early stages and had not hidden any troops. Nor had Ney yet received Napoleon's urgent request that he send the bulk of his force to Ligny. Instead two battles – at Ligny and Quatre Bras – developed simultaneously only about seven miles from each other. Ney had too often in the Peninsula seen the ill-effect of attacking British infantry head on, and quite possibly feared that the crossroads of Quatre Bras hid another Wellingtonian deception, in the way that in 1810 the use of topography had won him the battle of Busaco against Marshal Masséna.

Believing that Ney could manage to take Quatre Bras with the troops already under his command, Napoleon sent a message to General Drouet d'Erlon, who was on his way to reinforce Ney from Gosselies with the 1st Corps, to march to the battlefield of Ligny instead, where fierce house-to-house combat had developed. By 5 p.m. Blücher's force was hard-pressed, and he had to commit his reserves to the struggle, a dangerous moment for any commander when facing Napoleon. Had the French emperor been able to fling d'Erlon's fresh troops into the battle, a rout would have been assured. But no such force was there, not least because d'Erlon had been counter-ordered by Ney to march to Quatre Bras instead. As it was, d'Erlon arrived on neither battlefield in time to affect the outcome of either engagement. The greatest living authority on the campaigns of Napoleon, Dr David Chandler, has stated that the importance of the non-appearance of d'Erlon's corps at Ligny and Quatre Bras was crucial, since 'in either . . . its intervention could have been decisive'.[12]

By the time nightfall had descended on the battlefield of Quatre Bras it was clear that there was a stalemate, with both sides in much the same position they had occupied before Ney had originally attacked. Over 9,000 lives had been lost – roughly equally on each side – to no significant strategic advantage to either.

Yet over at Ligny a few miles to the east it was a very different picture. Even despite d'Erlon's non-appearance, Napoleon had conclusively given Blücher the damnable mauling that Wellington had predicted. The Emperor had delayed launching an attack by his Imperial Guard – the crack regiments nicknamed '*Les Invincibles*' – until 7.30 p.m., but when he had – preceded by a huge artillery bombardment – it had proved decisive. Crying '*Vive l'Empereur!*' the Guard had charged the Prussian centre with bayonets, supported by brigades of cavalry. Although Blücher personally counterattacked with only two brigades of cavalry, the French could not be turned back.

Darkness turned the defeat into a rout. Sixteen thousand Prussians were killed or wounded at Ligny, and around 8,000 Rhinelanders deserted the colours that night and simply returned home. Nonetheless the decision was taken by Blücher's chief of staff General August von Gneisenau – in Blücher's absence, because the marshal could not be found – that the army should act in a completely counter-intuitive way. Instead of retreating eastwards towards Liège and Prussia, the Prussians would instead go north to Wavre, where they could stay in touch with the Anglo-Allied army. Gneisenau was an Anglophobe, but he had nevertheless made the crucial decision of the campaign, one that Wellington himself hardly exaggerated when he described it as 'the decisive moment of the century'.

If Gneisenau had returned to Prussia, Wellington would probably have had to retreat north towards Antwerp and the Channel ports and probably re-embark the British army back to the United Kingdom, as had happened on so many other equally humiliating occasions over the past quarter-century. The Royal Navy were used to shipping defeated British forces back from a Napoleon-dominated Continent, and this time would have been no different. Yet with the Prussians still in the field, and liaising closely, there was still the prospect that they could pull off the coup that Napoleon missed at Ligny, that of bringing a fresh force onto the battlefield at the psychologically vital moment.

The Prussian retreat northward necessitated Wellington making a similar manoeuvre, giving up the crossroads that had been so hard fought over only the previous day. He could not risk having the combined forces of Napoleon and Ney fall upon him, so Saturday, 17 June was spent retreating to a highly defensible position some miles to the north, on the slopes of Mont St Jean, which – despite the best efforts of generations of French historians – will always be generally known as the battlefield of Waterloo. 'Old Blücher has had a damned good licking and gone back to Wavre, eighteen miles,' Wellington said. 'As he has gone back, we must go too. I suppose in England they'll say we have been licked. Well, I can't help it.' It had happened enough in the past; whenever Wellington had made tactical retreats in the Peninsula there had never been a shortage of those he termed 'croakers', especially among the radical Whigs in the parliamentary opposition, keen to suggest that he had been defeated.

The French, too, were happy to argue that Wellington had been 'licked'. Napoleon sent back a report of the battle of Ligny to be printed in the official government newspaper *Le Moniteur* which suggested that the united Prussian and Anglo-Allied armies had been defeated. The propaganda sheet duly obliged and there were celebrations in the French capital.

For a man responsible for several maxims about the importance of never losing a moment in wartime, Napoleon's relative inactivity on 17 June was almost inexplicable. He spent the day dictating letters, surveying the battlefield of Ligny and then breaking another of his favoured maxims by splitting his force just before a major engagement.

Napoleon detached his most recently-created marshal, Emmanuel de Grouchy, to follow the Prussians with 30,000 infantry and cavalry and ninety-six guns, a large force that he would desperately need the following day. The bad staff work and mutual misunderstandings that had ensured that d'Erlon had spent the previous day marching between battlefields without firing a shot further conspired to keep Grouchy away from Waterloo, where he might have made a huge difference. Added to inferior staff work was the inherently unimaginative personality of Grouchy himself. Only raised to the marshalate that April, he believed that 'inspiration in war is only appropriate to the commander-in-chief', and that 'lieutenants must confine themselves to executing orders'. So he interpreted Napoleon's orders to him in their most literal possible sense, and marched off towards Gembloux in the hope of harrying the Prussian rear and preventing Blücher from joining Wellington. (Blücher had meanwhile rejoined Gneisenau, having been concussed during a fall from his dead horse in the skirmishing at the end of Ligny.)

Any opportunity that Napoleon might have had to attack Wellington as he was withdrawing from Quatre Bras after ten o'clock on the morning of the seventeenth was passed up by him and Ney, and when Napoleon rejoined Ney there he shouted: 'You have ruined France!' With the rain making the transport of artillery tough going, the French army followed Wellington up the Charleroi–Brussels road, hoping for the opportunity of a decisive encounter before the Prussians – of whose exact whereabouts Napoleon (and indeed Grouchy) was uncertain – could regroup. It all came down to numbers and odds: Napoleon had a larger army than either Wellington or Blücher, but not larger than both of them combined.

The French followed hard on the heels of the withdrawing British, and a compelling narrative of the day was given by Captain Cavalié Mercer of the British horse artillery, whose memoirs of the campaign are a superb historical source. 'We galloped for our lives through the storm, straining to gain the enclosures about the houses of the hamlets,' wrote Mercer. 'Lord Uxbridge urging us on, crying, "Make haste! – Make haste! For God's sake gallop, or you will be taken!"' The thunderstorms that were developing – 'Flash succeeded flash, and the peals of thunder were long and tremendous' – put paid to French hopes of catching up with the Anglo-Allied rearguard, although there was an occasion at Genappe where the British Life Guards had to charge French lancers to cover the withdrawal, which they did successfully, 'sending their opponents flying in all directions'. There were a series of narrow escapes for the Anglo-Allied army retreating from Quatre Bras, which Mercer described as 'a fox hunt'.

The torrential downpour of 17 June continued until long after the Anglo-Allied rearguard had halted on the slopes of Mont St Jean, a few miles south of Waterloo. Those soldiers who did not have tents slept in their greatcoats, soaking wet. A British infantry private (later sergeant) named William Wheeler of the 51st Regiment recalled how 'We sat on our knapsacks until daylight without fires. The water ran in streams from the cuffs of our jackets, in short we were wet as if we were plunged overhead in a river. We had one consolation, we knew the enemy [was] in the same plight. The morning of the 18th June broke upon us and found us drenched with rain, benumbed and shaking with cold.' An officer later wrote that it seemed as if the water was being tumbled out of heaven in tubs.[13]

Charles O'Neil, a private in the 28th Regiment of Foot who had survived the terrible storming of Badajoz in the Peninsular War, recorded his memories of the night before the battle. A thief, deserter, fugitive and conman, O'Neil was not much given to sentimentality, but his account of the emotions of the night rings profoundly true:

I was just endeavouring to compose myself to sleep when my comrade spoke to me, saying that it was deeply impressed on his mind that he should not survive the morrow; and that he wished to make an arrangement with me, that if he should die and I should survive, I should inform his friends of the circumstances of his death, and that he would do the same for me, in case he should be the survivor. We then exchanged the last letters we had received from home, so that each should have the address of the other's parents. I endeavoured to conceal my own feelings, and cheer his, by reminding him that it was far better to die on the field of glory than from fear; but he turned away from me, and with a burst of tears, that spoke the deep feelings of his heart, he said, 'My mother!' The familiar sound of this precious name, and the sight of his sorrow, completely overcame my attempts at concealment, and we wept together.[14]

(Sure enough, although O'Neil himself was wounded at Waterloo, his comrade was killed twenty-five minutes into the action, and O'Neil duly informed the parents of the circumstances.)

Before daybreak, Wellington received a message that would make the gruelling night undergone by the British army wholly worthwhile. Blücher sent word that as soon as it was light enough to march, he would be sending not only Bülow's corps (which had not taken part in Ligny) to Wellington's aid, but two whole corps – virtually the entire Prussian army – leaving only one corps to guard Wavre against Grouchy coming up from Gembloux. This was about treble the numbers Wellington had been expecting and hoping for, and it completely altered his thinking about the battle that was clearly to be joined the next day.

Instead of merely a holding action in front of the large Forest of Soignes to his rear, through which there was only one road to Brussels, Wellington could now envisage doing to Napoleon what

Napoleon had hoped to do to the Prussians at Ligny: crush the enemy with a surprise eruption of extra troops onto its flank in the course of the battle.

For Napoleon had not the first hint of a suspicion that the Prussians, largely through the superhuman efforts of their commander, had been transformed in less than forty-eight hours from a defeated force fleeing the battlefield of Ligny into a disciplined army ready to take the offensive against the French once again. Meanwhile Grouchy, despite the large force at his disposal, had failed to make significant contact with the Prussian rearguard. He had also taken seven hours to march the six miles to Gembloux, which even in the torrential rain was a tortoise-like speed.

Napoleon desperately needed that force to be commanded by a marshal of dash and verve, but instead he had given the job to Grouchy. The most impressive cavalry commander in Europe, Napoleon's brother-in-law Joachim Murat, King of Naples, had fled Italy and offered his services, but the Emperor had turned him down. Marshal Davout was holding down the job of minister of war back in Paris, while Marshal Suchet was commanding the divisions guarding France's eastern approaches. Most of the other twenty-six marshals were either dead, had declared for the Bourbons, or were refusing to commit themselves to either side.

The knowledge that his left flank would be protected by the Prussians encouraged Wellington to strengthen the right and centre of his line. He also left over 17,000 men (3,000 British and 14,000 Dutch and Hanoverian) off the battlefield altogether, stationing them nine miles to the west at a village named Hal, under the joint commands of Prince Frederick of the Netherlands and Lieutenant-General Sir Charles Colville, who were both under the overall command of General Lord Hill. These troops would, Wellington hoped, be able to prevent any extravagant outflanking movement on the right flank, since he suspected that Napoleon might only be feinting at the Charleroi–Brussels road and really intended to march on Brussels via Mons.

Many historians – and not only historians: Napoleon himself fastened upon it – have criticised Wellington for leaving so large a force a two- or three-hour march away from the battlefield and for not recalling them the moment it became clear that Napoleon intended no large-scale manoeuvre but only a 'hard pounding' attack up the centre. They have even likened Wellington's detachment at Hal to Napoleon sending off Marshal Grouchy, thereby deliberately absenting a large body of men who could have been invaluable at the battle. In Wellington's defence the historian Jac Weller has argued that:

> On the morning of the eighteenth Wellington did not know the exact position of all French forces. He could see by personal observation that Napoleon had detached a considerable portion of his entire army. There were about 39,000 Frenchmen unaccounted for; he knew of Grouchy's movements in general, but not his strength. If Grouchy had only half this force, the other half could have been moving to turn the Duke's right flank. Wellington did not underrate Napoleon, he wanted to prevent the Emperor from winning by really doing the unexpected.[15]

On the all-important question of the numbers present at the battle, I propose to take those quoted in Mark Adkin's excellent book *The Waterloo Companion*, which as well as their innate scholarly worth are close to those of most of the other experts. After their losses of 17,500 men at Ligny and Quatre Bras, and Grouchy's detaching with 30,000 men, the French army under Napoleon comprised 53,400 infantry, 15,600 cavalry and 6,500 artillerymen servicing 246 guns, along with 2,000 support staff from medics to engineers, making a total of 77,500. After losing 4,500 at Quatre Bras, and stationing 17,000 at Hal, the Anglo-Allied army under Wellington comprised 53,800 infantry, 13,350 cavalry, 5,000 artillerymen servicing 157 guns and one rocket section, and 1,000 support staff, totalling 73,150 men. The Prussian troops available to assist Wellington if Blücher's plan was properly implemented consisted of 38,000 infantry, 7,000 cavalry, 2,500 artillerymen servicing 134 guns, and 1,500 support staff, totalling 49,000 men. Of the Prussian forces, IV Corps would arrive on the battlefield at about 4.30 p.m. with 31,000 men and eighty-six guns, II Corps would get there at about 6.30 p.m. with 12,800 men, and I Corps at around 7.30 p.m. with 5,000 men.

By the time the sun rose on the undulating plateau of Mont St Jean on Sunday, 18 June it was clear to everyone that there was going to be a major engagement that day – a battle on the scale of any of the great clashes of the Napoleonic Wars, such as Marengo, Friedland, Austerlitz, Borodino or Leipzig. 'Ah! Now I've got them, those English!' Napoleon is said to have exclaimed when he was certain that the Anglo-Allied army had not filed away down the road through the Forest of Soignes during the night. He later expressed incredulity that Wellington had fought with an impassable forest to his rear, but in fact Wellington did this on purpose. 'It is not true that I could not have retreated,' he told his friend Harriet Arbuthnot eight years later. 'I could have got into the wood and I would have defied the Devil to drive me out.'[16]

Napoleon underlined his extreme optimism at a breakfast meeting with his senior commanders held in the farmhouse of Le Caillou, on the Charleroi–Brussels road, where he had spent the previous night. 'We have ninety chances in our favour,' he crowed, 'and not ten against.' General Maximilien Foy tried to warn the Emperor of the likely steadfastness of the British line, saying: 'The time has come when an old soldier feels it is his duty to remind Your Majesty that while the Duke of Wellington's position is one that he cannot contemplate for permanent occupation, you are now in front of an infantry which, during the whole of the Spanish war, I never saw give way.' Marshal Soult, who had also spent years in the Peninsula, supported Foy, but Napoleon was quick to pooh-pooh them. 'Just because you have been beaten by Wellington,' he told them, 'you think he's a good general. But I tell you that Wellington is a bad general and the English are bad troops.' The whole business would be, he assured them, *'l'affaire d'un déjeuner'* (a picnic).[17] Instead it turned out to be perhaps the most famous battle of world history.

THE BATTLE

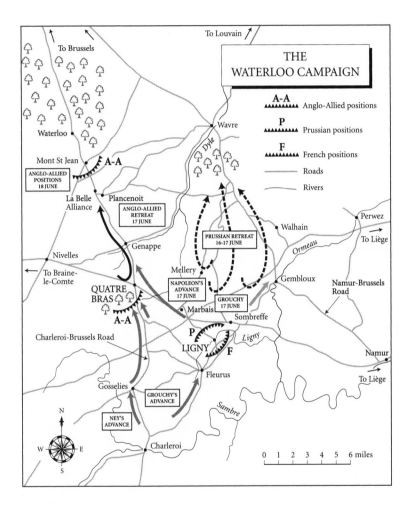

The Waterloo Campaign
Taken from J.C. Herold, *The Battle of Waterloo* (Cassell, 1967), p.69

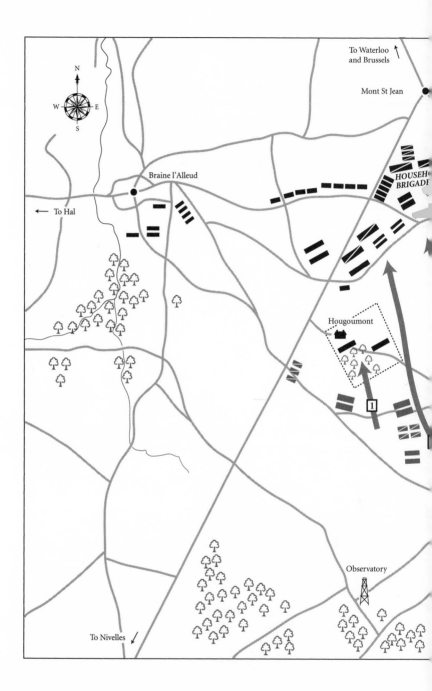

The Battle of Waterloo
Herold, ibid., p.125

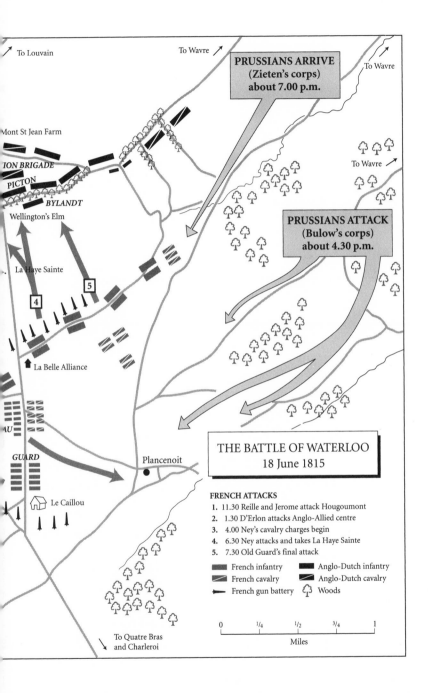

To Louvain

To Wavre

PRUSSIANS ARRIVE
(Zieten's corps)
about 7.00 p.m.

To Wavre

Mont St Jean Farm

ION BRIGADE

To Wavre

PRUSSIANS ATTACK
(Bulow's corps)
about 4.30 p.m.

PICTON

BYLANDT

Wellington's Elm

La Haye Sainte

5

4

La Belle Alliance

AU

GUARD

Plancenoit

Le Caillou

THE BATTLE OF WATERLOO
18 June 1815

FRENCH ATTACKS
1. 11.30 Reille and Jerome attack Hougoumont
2. 1.30 D'Erlon attacks Anglo-Allied centre
3. 4.00 Ney's cavalry charges begin
4. 6.30 Ney attacks and takes La Haye Sainte
5. 7.30 Old Guard's final attack

French infantry	Anglo-Dutch infantry
French cavalry	Anglo-Dutch cavalry
French gun battery	Woods

To Quatre Bras
and Charleroi

0   ¼   ½   ¾   1

Miles

1

The First Phase

WELLINGTON HAD CHOSEN his ground well. As he looked southwards from his vantage point under an elm tree at the crossroads of the Ohain road towards the French army on the morning of the battle he would have seen two buildings, each of which was to play a key role in the coming events. To his centre-right in an advanced position were the château and outbuildings of Hougoumont, well protected with walls, ditches, hedges and surrounded by a wood, which the Duke had invested with his best troops of all, the British Foot Guards (along with some Nassauers, Hanoverians and Lüneburgers), with orders to hold the place come what might. That they succeeded in this, despite heavy and repeated attacks by the French infantry, was one of the keys to Wellington's victory at Waterloo.

Over to his centre-left was La Haye Sainte, another well-defended farmhouse with stables, a barn and a piggery, all enclosed by high walls, which Wellington filled with the King's German Legion, the émigré unit loyal to King George III which had demonstrated its first-class fighting abilities during the Peninsular War. The possession of these two strongholds, with their high brick walls, would prove invaluable in disrupting the French line of advance, because, as one historian put it, 'no enemy could pass without being assailed in flank by musketry'.[1]

The two armies – separated by a shallow valley – were only a thousand yards or so apart as they cooked their breakfasts on the morning of the battle (Hougoumont was much closer, only 400 yards from the enemy front line). In the distance, behind the French lines, Wellington could make out the red-tiled, white-walled farmhouse of La Belle Alliance, the appositely named inn that was to play a romantic role in the battle's epilogue. On his far left were three more walled and well-defended buildings, the farms of Papelotte and La Haye and the château of Frischermont.

Howell Rees Gronow, a Welsh Old Etonian ensign who was on duty with the 1st Regiment of Foot Guards at St James's Palace when the Waterloo campaign began, skipped his guard duty there hoping to see action at Waterloo and to return before anyone noticed he was missing. On the morning of the battle, he recalled:

> We had not proceeded a quarter of a mile when we heard the trampling of horses' feet, and on looking round perceived a large cavalcade of officers coming at full speed. In a moment we recognised the Duke himself at their head . . . The entire staff of the army was close at hand . . . They all seemed as gay and unconcerned as if they were riding to meet the hounds in some quiet English county.[2]

They had good reason to be confident, if not quite 'gay and unconcerned', because the topography across which Wellington had chosen to receive Napoleon's attacks could hardly have been better suited for infantry, complete with folds and dips in the ground that could shelter defenders against the artillery bombardment of a far larger force of cannon – Napoleon had 246 to Wellington's 157. Sergeant-Major Edward Cotton of the 7th Hussars discoursed upon 'the principal advantages' of Wellington's position, which had much to recommend it besides the two defensible buildings, including factors that – due to the lie of the ground – would not have been visible to Napoleon:

> The juncture of the two high-roads immediately in rear of our centre, from which branched off the paved road to Brussels, our main line of communication . . . added to the facility of communication, and enabled us to move ammunition, guns, troops, the wounded, etc, to or from any part of our main front line, as circumstances demanded . . . the continuous ridge from flank to flank towards which no hostile force could advance undiscovered, within range of our artillery upon the crest. Behind this ridge our troops could manoeuvre, or lie concealed from the enemy's view, while they were in great measure protected from the fire of the hostile batteries . . . Our extreme left was strong by nature. The buildings, hollow-ways, enclosures, trees and brushwood, along the valley from Papelotte to Ohain, thickly peopled with light infantry, would have kept a strong force long at bay . . . Our extreme right was secured by numerous patches of brushwood, trees and ravines, and further protected by hamlets.[3]

Two other vital aspects to the battlefield need to be borne in mind: the corn that grew up to chest, and in some fields shoulder, height and which could hide bodies of troops and slow down advances; and the glutinous mud which also retarded movement.

The rain had cleared by about nine o'clock on the morning of Sunday the eighteenth, but the ground was still very muddy from the previous day and night's downpours. Dennis Wheeler, a climatologist at the University of Sunderland, has recently recreated a weather map of the low-pressure ridge that moved over the battlefield for about forty-eight hours before the fighting began, and has described the rain as 'apocalyptic'.

When Napoleon was informed by General Drouot, Adjutant-

General of the Imperial Guard, that the artillery needed firmer ground before it could be properly deployed, he made his next major error. Since he had no idea that the Prussians were back on the offensive, and were even then marching towards him from Wavre, he believed that time was on his side, rather than its being a precious but fast-diminishing commodity.

So when at the breakfast conference Jérôme Bonaparte had said that the waiter serving him the previous day had overheard Wellington saying that the Prussians would arrive in front of the Forest of Soignes, Napoleon merely scoffed at his youngest brother, dismissing the information out of hand. Shakespeare would easily have recognised the role that hubris and arrogance played in Napoleon's downfall.

To haul a twelve-pounder cannon – so called because of the weight of shot it fired, nearly a stone of lead per round – up a slope, in mud, was no mean undertaking; and Napoleon's Grand Battery at Waterloo constituted sixty guns and twenty howitzers. Yet the demands of Drouot and the artillery experts that the ground be allowed to dry first – which sounded only sensible to someone who had learnt his military trade as a gunner – meant that Napoleon squandered his chance for an early assault on the Anglo-Allied army before the Prussians arrived on the scene.

The late start was not entirely the Emperor's fault. His army took far longer to assemble than was originally envisaged, coming up from their sodden sleeping areas and bivouacs sometimes miles from the battlefield. Many troops had been dispersed to forage for food and shelter in the downpour, and the mud delayed the forming up of units on the battlefield. Of course, had Napoleon had an inkling of the proximity of the Prussians, none of this would have been allowed to preclude a dawn attack.

Another effect of the heavy rainfall of the night of 17–18 June that worked against Napoleon was the way that it softened the ground, to the extent that cannonballs tended to plough into the mud, rather than bounce along hardened ground. A cannonball fired at sun-baked ground might bounce as many as five or six times, leaving death and carnage in its wake, while one that merely buried itself after its initial impact had only a fraction of that lethal capacity. Tests undertaken by the Royal Artillery in 2003 proved how diminished were Napoleon's batteries' effectiveness by the downpour the night before the battle.

While Napoleon could hardly have ordained good weather, he did make serious blunders of his own for which he must take ultimate blame. Instead of ordering Grouchy to return to the scene as soon as possible, at 10 a.m. on 17 June Napoleon had sent him orders to march on Wavre and engage the Prussians, orders which could only have the effect of forcing them closer towards junction with Wellington. Several of Napoleon's written orders during the campaign were unclear or contradictory – his handwriting was, moreover, akin to the meanderings of an intoxicated spider – but these instructions were particularly strategically inept.

At only three miles wide by one and a half deep, Waterloo was a very small battlefield by Napoleonic standards, especially for a total of over 180,000 men to fight in. Napoleon's tactical options were therefore severely limited, since Wellington had effectively closed down large areas of the battlefield to him. The huge flanking movements that Napoleon often favoured were effectively blocked off, to the east by the well-defended farm buildings of the hamlets of Papelotte, La Haye and Frischermont and to the west by the village of Braine l'Alleud. Napoleon therefore decided upon a frontal assault with a couple of mild diversions, which was hardly an inspired tactic, but was perhaps all that was open to him given the terrain.

Since the horrifically expensive battle of Borodino outside Moscow in 1812 Napoleon had inured himself to the terrible losses inherent in frontal assaults, and the French death toll at Waterloo showed that he had not altered his thinking during his brief exile on Elba. Put at its most basic, his plan was simply to break the enemy's centre, gain possession of the slopes of Mont St Jean and thus split Wellington's army in half while controlling the all-important road to Brussels. He reckoned without the steadiness under attack of the British infantry that Wellington had largely deployed in the centre, perhaps because he had never personally fought against the British since he captured Toulon from the Royal Navy nearly two decades previously.

Napoleon's supposed ill-health has frequently been used by historians – more often than not, French historians – to explain away the Emperor's comparative lack of imagination in his plan for the battle. He has been diagnosed (by historians rather than by contemporary doctors) as suffering from a disease called acromegaly, a disorder of the pituitary gland, which induces a combination of torpor and over-confidence.[4] Inflammation of the bladder and urinary tract has also been attributed to him, and he certainly had suffered from it in the past, but he had been in generally good health – though overweight – on Elba. According to his brother Jérôme and his surgeon Baron Larrey, Napoleon suffered from haemorrhoids the night after Ligny, which Larrey and the Emperor's valet Louis Marchand attended to with warm, clean, wet flannels. They were obviously successful in this, because the Emperor spent several hours in the saddle on 17 and 18 June, something that would have been quite impossible otherwise.

He was certainly in the saddle when at about 9 a.m., in order to enthuse his men and perhaps to try to intimidate the enemy, as well as to kill time while the ground hardened, Napoleon rode along the whole of the front line. It also allowed him to inspect the enemy's position for the third time since midnight. The bands played, the soldiers cried '*Vive l'Empereur!*', and the spectacle was undoubtedly an imposing one as the Man of Destiny, as he occasionally referred to himself, showed himself to his troops and they to him.

It is a curious fact about the battle of Waterloo that no one is absolutely certain when it actually began. Historians dispute the exact timing, because the men whose lives were at stake did not bother to synchronise or check their watches for our benefit, having more pressing things to do. No historian denies, however, that the first phase began with a massive bombardment from the Grand Battery and an attack by General Reille's corps upon Hougoumont.*

Just as the Grand Battery was opening up, at around 11.30 a.m., a corporal from the 2nd Silesian Hussars, a Prussian cavalry regiment, was captured in the Bois de Paris by French cavalry. He quickly divulged the vital information that his unit was merely the advance guard for Blücher's army, which was making its way towards the battlefield. Nor was this the first indication that the French had of what was afoot: as early as 9.30 a.m. the Prussian Graf von Schwerin had been killed by a shot from a French horse artillery battery.

Eleven-thirty in the morning was thus the point at which

---

* The practice of dividing Waterloo into five distinct but overlapping phases was begun by Sir James Shaw Kennedy, who took part in the battle, has been followed by later historians such as Captain A.F. Becke, Sir John Keegan, Elizabeth Longford and Ian Fletcher, and is still easily the best way of making sense of it.

Napoleon, who had scarcely by then even initiated it, ought to have broken off the engagement and retreated to fight on ground of his own rather than Wellington's choosing. Perhaps considering the information might be faulty, or that he would have plenty of time later to review his options, or most likely in the belief that he could defeat Wellington before Blücher arrived, Napoleon decided to press on with the attack on Hougoumont. (Many of the most sophisticated of the modern war-gaming techniques played on the battle regularly demonstrate that it was nigh-impossible for Napoleon to have won Waterloo without first capturing Hougoumont, because its continued possession by Wellington stymies the French 'player' from executing any imaginative moves against the Anglo-Allied right or centre-right.)

Hougoumont was situated some 500 yards in front of Wellington's line along the crest of the ridge, meaning that it could disrupt any general French advance. Reille's assault at roughly 11.30 a.m. was only intended as a diversion, with the hope that Wellington would have to weaken his line by sending in reserves to reinforce the heavily-pressed farmhouse. Not only did this not happen, but the very reverse became the case: it was the French who steadily poured more and more troops into the effort to take Hougoumont, which continued throughout the day. A serious attempt to take the farmhouse would have required heavy artillery fire against the gate and walls, which for some reason was not employed. Napoleon never rode over towards Hougoumont during the course of the battle; had he done so he would immediately have spotted the vast numbers of Jérôme's troops that were being committed to the struggle to capture the château. The generally stationary position he adopted, in great contrast to Wellington's highly peripatetic approach to command, worked against the Emperor.

The siege was only finally raised when the rest of the French army had been repulsed from the slopes of Mont St Jean, and the defence by a collection of Coldstream Guards, 3rd Foot (later Scots) Guards, 900 Nassauers, a Brunswick battalion and two companies of the 1st (later Grenadier) Guards was heroic. It is estimated that the 2,600 Anglo-Allied troops at Hougoumont occupied the attentions of 12,700 Frenchmen for much of this vital 'battle within a battle'.

At one point a detachment of thirty French troops from the 1st Light Infantry managed to enter the farmhouse, led by a huge Frenchman nicknamed '*l'Enforceur*' who was armed with an axe, but Lieutenant-Colonel James Macdonnell, along with nine others including Corporals James and Joseph Graham of the Coldstream Guards, managed to close the gate again and the Frenchmen were all massacred save for a fourteen-year-old drummer boy. When many years later a bequest was made in a vicar's will 'to the bravest man in the British army at Waterloo', Wellington – who was asked to nominate the beneficiary – stated that 'the success of the battle turned upon closing the gates at Hougoumont', and so Corporal James Graham, by then a sergeant, was tracked down with the help of Macdonnell and awarded the money.

Cotton recorded how some time after the gates had been closed, Graham had

> asked permission to fall out for a few minutes, a request which surprised Colonel Macdonnell, and induced him to inquire the motive. Graham replied that his brother was lying in the buildings wounded, and, as the flames were then fast extending, he wished to remove him to a place of safety. The request was granted, and Graham, having rescued his brother from the fate which menaced him, speedily returned to his post.[5]

(James Graham died an inmate of the Royal Hospital, Kilmainham, in 1845.)

If the gates had been forced open for long enough there can be little doubt that all those caught inside the perimeter would have been killed. Of all the emotionally moving places on today's battlefield – at least for a Briton – Hougoumont is the most powerfully evocative, with its wall plaques, gravestones, chapel and the loopholes in the walls through which the Guards wreaked such havoc on the French attacking through the adjacent wood. Byron etched his name on the walls when he visited the following year. (When visiting it is important to remember that the walls of the farmhouse were higher in 1815 than they are today.)

Hougoumont's defenders were aided by Wellington's order to Captain Robert Bull to fire howitzers at the wood from which the French, having taken it expensively from the Nassau and Hanoverian infantry, were beginning to emerge. The slaughter outside the walls as the French tried unsuccessfully to scale them was appalling. Later in the day howitzers were deployed by the French, which set fire to the château itself and to other outbuildings, but the Guards continued defending the walled garden and were never dislodged from it. Many are the tales of valour from Hougoumont, on both sides, and the story of its defence is not unlike that of Rorke's Drift in the Zulu War.

A message that Wellington sent Macdonnell during the assault illustrates the desperation of the situation once the French howitzers had done their job:

> I can see that the fire has communicated from the hay stack to the roof of the chateau. You must however still keep your men in those parts to which the fire does not reach. Take care that no men are lost by the falling in of the roof, or floors: after they will have fallen in occupy the ruined

walls inside of the garden; particularly if it should be possible
for the enemy to pass through the embers in the inside of
the house.[6]

The fighting at Hougoumont sucked in more and more French
troops throughout the day. 'No troops but the British could
have held Hougoumont, and only the best of them at that,' was
Wellington's encomium to the defenders. After the battle, in the
hearing of Ensign Gronow, Major-General Peregrine Maitland
told Lord Saltoun, whose 1st Foot Guards had held the orchard
of Hougoumont: 'Your defence saved the army: nothing could be
more gallant. Every man of you deserves promotion.' Saltoun
replied that it had been 'touch and go – a matter of life and
death – for all within the walls had sworn that they would never
surrender'. Saltoun's adjutant added, 'Our officers were determined never to yield, and the men were resolved to stand by them
to the last.'[7]

The attacks on Hougoumont continued at various levels of
intensity for over eight hours, but at about 1.30 p.m. a second
phase of the battle opened up when, after a bombardment by the
French artillery, General d'Erlon was given his second opportunity
to affect the course of the campaign.

2

The Second Phase

MUCH OF THE ART of warfare in the Napoleonic era
depended not on the technology of weaponry, which had
altered very little since the wars of Marlborough, but upon the
skilled interaction of the three main military elements of the day:
cavalry, infantry and artillery. When these were deployed in a
coordinated way, complementing and supporting each other in
attack and anchoring each other in defence, they could be a
formidable, indeed campaign-winning juggernaut. Yet time and
again in the battle of Waterloo the French strategists, by which
must principally be meant Napoleon, his chief of staff Marshal
Soult and his battlefield commander Marshal Ney, failed to
employ the three arms to their best advantage.

Each of the three arms had its own strengths and weaknesses
in terms of manoeuvrability, firepower and offensive potential.
A regiment of infantry that had formed itself into a square
was almost impregnable to a conventional cavalry charge, but
highly vulnerable to an artillery bombardment or the volleying
of another infantry unit formed in line, while cavalry charging
cannon could do so in a quarter of the time that infantry could,
with consequently fewer losses. Artillery meanwhile employed
different kinds of shot for different tasks. The key in a fast-
changing battle was to deploy each arm in such a way as to

play to its strengths and to support the achievements of the other two. This simply did not happen much on the French side at Waterloo, but was a crucial factor in Wellington's flexible defence.

Napoleon hoped that after half an hour of cannonading his Grand Battery would have so weakened the Anglo-Allied left-centre that a frontal assault by d'Erlon's corps marching in column would be able to punch a hole in Wellington's line. Yet because, in part, of Wellington's technique of deploying his men behind the crest of the slopes, sometimes even lying down, the death toll amongst the Anglo-Allied infantry was nothing like what it had been for the more visible Prussian troops at Ligny.

A nine- or twelve-pound cannonball fired at high velocity was a terrifying thing: the momentum created by its speed and weight made it capable of ploughing through massed ranks of men, tightly packed together as they were according to the tactics of the day. Several are the stories of men putting out a foot to halt what they thought was a slowly rolling, spent cannonball only to discover that it still had the ability to smash through bone and flesh. Even after a ball had bounced several times, each time roughly half the distance of the last, depending on how hard the ground was, it was still a lethal weapon. Yet unlike howitzers, cannonballs needed a straight trajectory, and with many of Wellington's men hidden, the Grand Battery was denied one.

When, however, as happened to the 27th (Inniskilling) Regiment, the French artillery could directly pound an Anglo-Allied unit, the result was utter carnage. John Kincaid, one of the officers of the 95th Regiment stationed nearby in what, because it had been used to extract gravel, was called 'the Sandpit', wrote of how 'The Twenty-Seventh regiment were lying literally dead, in square, a few yards behind us. I had never yet heard of a battle in which everybody was killed; but this seems likely to be an exception, as all were going by turns.'

By 1.30 p.m. Napoleon knew for certain that the black-clad troops who were emerging in ever greater numbers from the woods on the east of the battlefield were not, as he had initially hoped, Grouchy's corps come to win the day by staving in Wellington's left flank, but rather von Bülow's Prussians intent on doing the same thing to his own right flank. Since he did not know how many Prussians would be emanating from that theatre of operations, and presumably hoped that Grouchy had bottled up a large proportion of Blücher's force, he sent off only part of his cavalry reserve – under Generals Domon, Subervie and Lobau – to observe the situation.

It was now clear that time was no longer on his side, so at 1.30 p.m. the Emperor launched what he hoped would be an invincible infantry assault, as large an attack as any of the Napoleonic Wars. D'Erlon's corps numbered around 16,000 men, over a quarter of Napoleon's entire army at Waterloo; a tremendous force to launch at the centre-left of the Anglo-Allied line. Had it broken through there can be little doubt that Napoleon would have won the day, since with the forest at his back Wellington would have had no room to manoeuvre his army together as a single unit again. Halting and reversing the mass of men as they marched towards Wellington's line, their drums beating and flags flying, was therefore of the utmost importance.

The uneven ground which the corps had to traverse, about 1,300 yards of it, moreover in places allowed some cover to the French troops. To walk the ground of d'Erlon's advance today takes some fifteen to twenty minutes, even without the six-foot-high corn and the mud underfoot that slowed his troops then. In

1815 it must have taken just as long, if not longer, an excruciating time to advance under cannon-fire.

There is still much debate among historians as to the exact formation that d'Erlon chose for his four divisions to press home the attack. It has given rise to the accusation that the French commanders, by choosing a column rather than a line formation, were myopic and clumsy. This cannot necessarily be levelled at Napoleon himself, who could not be expected to have attended to such a detail in person, so much as at Ney as the battlefield commander and d'Erlon as the corps commander, and possibly also the four divisional commanders – Donzelot, Quiot, Marcognet and Durutte. D'Erlon's corps was protected by cavalry on both its flanks, but the problem would come from the centre.

It appears from the account we have from one of the captains who took part in the assault, a veteran named Duthilt, that the divisions attacked not in single columns but divisional columns formed up in battalions of three ranks each with 130 or so men in each, eight groups of three ranks each per division. A new and unfamiliar formation, it would doubtless have been greatly distorted during the march forward, but it was probably better in terms of firepower than the formations so often turned back in the Peninsular War, in which d'Erlon, Ney, Soult and several of the divisional commanders had all fought. Yet it is not by any means certain that this was in fact the formation adopted.

Eighty years ago, the historian Captain A.F. Becke put forward the intriguing theory that an order was garbled from 'colonne de battailon par divisions' into 'colonne de division par battailon', and that this perhaps accounted for what happened; but since the mass column had been used in the battles of Friedland and Wagram it is possible that d'Erlon actually intended to attack in old-fashioned column. Certainly, the tactics of the Napoleonic Wars altered very little during their course. Whatever the formation ultimately chosen, however, it was disastrous. British infantry had been formed in line to fight advancing French columns for six years in the Peninsula, and they had rarely lost. 'Napoleon did not manoeuvre at all,' said Wellington after Waterloo. 'He just moved forward in the old style, in columns, and was driven off in the old style.'[1]

D'Erlon managed some initial successes: Durutte succeeded in capturing the hamlet of Papelotte, and Donzelot diverted a brigade of his division to try to seize La Haye Sainte from the King's German Legion, taking its garden and orchard. A German infantry battalion that was sent to support Major Georg Baring in that very isolated position was badly cut up by a cuirassiers brigade on d'Erlon's left flank. If Donzelot had been supported by enough artillery to blow a breach in the wall of La Haye Sainte, or to set the place on fire, it might have been disastrous for Wellington's centre at that still early stage of the battle, but this basic act of forethought had not been carried out, as with so many others in the area of inter-arm communication on the French side.

One of the Frenchmen marching towards the British lines in d'Erlon's corps was Captain Duthilt, who had fought since the Revolutionary Wars and therefore had twenty-two years' experience of leading men in battle. He was concerned about several factors in the attack, massive though it was. The strength of Wellington's defences, the muddiness underfoot, the strange formation chosen for the corps by the generals, and the way in which the men's zealotry had been built up too early, all left him worried.[2] 'This rush and enthusiasm were becoming too disastrous,' the veteran recorded in his memoirs, admittedly with hindsight, 'in that the soldier still had a long march to make before meeting the enemy, and was soon tired out by the difficulty of manoeuvring on this heavy churned up soil, which ripped off gaiter straps and even lost shoes ... there was soon disorder in the ranks, above all as the head of the column came within range of enemy fire.'[3]

D'Erlon's men must be given credit for reaching the very crest of the slope on the Anglo-Allied left-centre, despite the heavy and accurate fire they were soaking up as they marched up the low ridge. To make matters worse for them there was a thick, six-foot-high hedge at the top, but in places they passed both that and the sunken road behind. When they reached von Bijlandt's Dutch-Belgian brigade it broke and ran, fleeing past Major-General Sir Thomas Picton's 5th Division. Although the brigade has occasionally been excoriated for cowardice, it ought to be recalled that it had been badly mauled at Quatre Bras, was therefore severely under-strength, had already withstood ninety minutes' cannonading at short range, and above all was not made up of men whose hearts were in the fight politically, ideologically or racially. If d'Erlon had been capable of consolidating his position on the crest of the ridge he could have turned Wellington's flank. A crisis of the battle was at hand.

D'Erlon also had the satisfaction of forcing some companies of the 95th Rifle Brigade – whose firepower was far more accurate over far longer distances owing to its employment of Baker rifles rather than muskets – out of the Sandpit to join the rest of their battalion behind the Wavre road. (It is an interesting fact of the Napoleonic Wars that other than the rifling of gun-barrels – which was in its infancy and which had the disadvantage of making reloading slower – there had been hardly any technological advance in firearms since the campaigns of Marlborough. The

Brown Bess musket had been introduced in 1745, and a *grognard* of the Wars of Spanish Succession would have been perfectly at home working the muskets of 1815.) The fleeing Dutch and Belgians of von Bijlandt's brigade fortunately had no effect on the morale of Picton's 5th Division as it prepared to meet the onslaught of d'Erlon's corps. The 5th was composed of the brigades of Major-General Sir James Kempt and Major-General Sir Denis Pack and Colonel von Vincke's Hanoverian brigade. Of the 5,170 men who had marched out of Brussels with it two days earlier, no fewer than 1,569 had been lost at Quatre Bras. The remaining 3,600 – supported by two Hanoverian brigades to their left with a total of 5,000 men – faced a far larger number of Frenchmen. Yet this did not prevent General Picton, after his troops had fired a murderous volley at about one hundred yards' range, from ordering a bayonet charge.

Picton himself was killed almost immediately afterwards, shot through the right temple with the words 'Charge! Charge! Hurrah!' on his lips, as the brigades of Donzelot and Quiot clashed with Kempt's, Marcognet's with Pack's, and Durutte attempted to deal with the Hanoverians.[4] (It was only after Picton's body was laid out at Brussels the day after the battle that it was discovered that he had received a severe contusion at Quatre Bras on 16 June that he had kept secret.)

'Ninety-second, everything has given way on your right and left and you must charge this column!' cried Pack. With cheers the 92nd Regiment – which had been reduced to only 220 men – responded to the call. The fixing of the bayonet is the work of a moment, and as one British officer recalled, 'When the Scots Greys charged past the flanks of the 92nd, both regiments cheered, and joined in the heart-touching cry of "Scotland forever!"' For it was at this key psychological moment, when d'Erlon's advance had seemed to lose its momentum, that Lord Uxbridge ordered a mass cavalry attack upon it.

Uxbridge had had a difficult relationship with Wellington ever since he had run away with Wellington's sister-in-law (whom he did at least subsequently marry). Wellington nevertheless appreciated his abilities and appointed him to command the cavalry in the Waterloo campaign, albeit with the joke to another officer: 'I'll take good care he doesn't run away with me!'[5] Uxbridge had served with distinction under Sir John Moore in the Peninsula, but had to give up the command of the cavalry when Wellington arrived there. This was to be the first time the two men had served together since the scandal. Apart from Wellington's refusal to discuss his plans for the battle with his second-in-command, merely letting drop a few semi-sarcastic remarks, they got on well enough.

Wellington had been harsh about the cavalry arm in the Peninsula, once accusing it of 'galloping at everything' without proper thought to the consequences, and the charge of the Union and Household Brigades at Waterloo also gave him opportunity for criticism. At the moment of the initial attack on d'Erlon, however, Uxbridge's action met with superb success as it charged through gaps in the hedge and around it to fall upon the French infantry.

The French cavalry protecting d'Erlon's corps on its left flank were swept away by the Household Brigade. Now, totally exposed and caught by surprise, d'Erlon's corps reeled from the combined onslaught of Picton's division, Major-General Sir William Ponsonby's Union Brigade (Royals, Scots Greys and Inniskillings dragoons) and, after their attack on the French cuirassiers, Lord Edward Somerset's Household Brigade (1st and 2nd Life Guards and Royal Horse Guards). Uxbridge himself took the head of Somerset's force. Within minutes d'Erlon's men had broken and run back down the slope, utterly demoralised and leaving 2,000 prisoners behind them. Two 'eagle' standards were captured, even though they were prized so highly in the French army as to have attained almost mythical status. Sergeant Charles Ewart of the 2nd North British Dragoons ('Scots Greys') captured the eagle of the 45th Line Regiment (Marcognet's division), and Captain Alexander Clark-Kennedy of the Royal Dragoons took that of the 105th (Quiot's division). (A third, that of the 55th Regiment, was also taken, but was recaptured soon afterwards.)

Sergeant Ewart later recalled how he captured the coveted French standard:

> I took the Eagle from the enemy: he and I had a hard contest for it; he thrust for my groin – I parried it off, and I cut him through the head: after which I was attacked by one of their Lancers, who threw his lance at me, but missed the mark by throwing it off with my sword by my right side; then I cut him from the chin upwards, which cut went through his teeth. Next I was attacked by a foot soldier, who, after firing at me, charged me with his bayonet; but he very soon lost the combat, for I parried it, and cut him down through the head; so that finished the combat for the Eagle.[6]

This was the point at which the British cavalry ought to have stopped, regrouped and returned to their posts. For many, however, this was their first battle experience, and instead, exhilarated by their success over d'Erlon's corps, they disastrously charged onwards. In a sense, therefore, Uxbridge did indeed 'run away' with Wellington, or at least with a good proportion of his cavalry arm. Although they had some success in cutting down some gunners of the Grand Battery, Ponsonby's Union Brigade went far beyond the point that the rest of the Anglo-Allied army was able to protect them. Despite Ponsonby and his staff's efforts they could not halt their troops. It was said that one officer was heard to cry out 'To Paris!' as he charged by.

French retribution was swift and merciless; spotting their opportunity, Jacquinot's lancers and Farine's cuirassiers attacked from both right and left and exacted a terrible toll on the British cavalry, killing or wounding one-third of their number. Ponsonby himself paid for his inability to rein back his over-enthusiastic troopers with his life, killed by a French lancer after he had surrendered.

Although Somerset's Household Brigade also went on too far after dispersing d'Erlon's corps, it reined in long before Ponsonby had done. The cavalry retreat was covered by Major-General Sir John Vandeleur's 4th Cavalry Brigade and Ghigny's Belgian and Dutch Light Dragoons, who managed to repulse bodies of French lancers that were chasing troopers of the Scots Greys back to the British lines. Of the 2,500 cavalry who had charged, over a thousand did not return.

Captain Tomkinson of the 16th Light Dragoons recorded the destruction in his *Diary of a Cavalry Officer*:

> Towards the close of the evening the whole brigade did not form above one squadron ... There was one squadron of the 1st Dragoon Guards in which not above one or two returned. They rode completely into the enemy's reserve, and were killed. The enemy, I suspect, did not spare a single prisoner who fell into their hands. It is impossible to suppose a whole squadron killed without one man surrendering.[7]

Although the aftermath had been disastrous – the Union Brigade's remaining strength meant that it could not contribute further as a functioning unit – nonetheless d'Erlon had been completely and demoralisingly repulsed, and had lost a quarter of his men, with around 2,000 captured. Napoleon's original plan of how to achieve victory had been foiled. With the struggle continuing over Hougoumont, and La Haye Sainte still in Major Baring's hands, if only just, Napoleon had not so far managed to impose his will upon any section of the battlefield. Meanwhile the Prussians were arriving in ever-increasing numbers from the east, directed to the vital points by Wellington's Prussian liaison officer, the redoubtable Baron Philipp von Müffling.

Nor had Picton's 5th Division succumbed to the same hubristic temptation as the cavalry. After their bayonet charge they obeyed orders to return to their line on the crest of the slope on the Anglo-Allied centre-left, thereby closing any gaps that Napoleon might have exploited if they had – maddened by blood-lust – followed d'Erlon's corps to the bottom of the slope and beyond. Three companies of the 95th returned to the Sandpit. Even the success of Durutte was reversed when Prince Bernhard's troops retook the farm of Papelotte.

At this point in the battle, soon after 3 p.m., there seems to have been a relative lull in the hostilities – except at the hard-pressed farmhouses – while both armies drew breath. Wellington used this short respite to bring General Sir John Lambert's 10th Brigade into the line where the von Bijlandt brigade had been, as Kempt took over from Picton as commander of the 5th Division.

Wellington certainly needed every moment; he had expected the Prussians to begin arriving at noon, but it was not really until after 4 p.m. that they could be deployed in large enough numbers to aid him significantly. Thankfully though, by that time the sound of Blücher's cannon could be clearly heard in the east.

Meanwhile Napoleon finally received a reply from Grouchy, which had been sent from Walhain on the Gembloux–Wavre road at 11 a.m. This stated that he was heading for Wavre, but was still some way off. The story goes that he was eating strawberries with some of his senior commanders at a farm on the road when the roar of the Grand Battery's guns was heard a few miles to the west. His subordinates, especially General Gérard, implored him to give up the Prussian chase and march immediately towards the sound of the guns, which could only mean that Napoleon was engaging the Anglo-Allied army.

Fearing the consequences of directly contravening the Emperor's verbal and written orders, Grouchy overruled them and insisted upon continuing the march on to Wavre. An officer with more initiative or imagination – Kellermann, say, or Pajol – would almost certainly have behaved differently, but Napoleon had given Grouchy his marshal's baton in the knowledge that he was not of that particular stamp. Grouchy's message made it clear to Napoleon that he would not be appearing on the battlefield that day, just as the charge of the Heavy and Union Brigades had dispersed any lingering suspicions he might have had that Wellington was merely fighting a rearguard action while he withdrew his main force through the Forest of Soignes.

With the Prussians starting to arrive in force from about 4.30 p.m. onwards, this was the time when the French could have – indeed should have – ended their attacks and gone onto the defensive. By withdrawing to a safe distance to await Grouchy's arrival the next day, Napoleon might have salvaged his throne, at least for a little while longer. Yet he was a gambler; his career had seen him escape from tough spots time and again, often merely by upping the stakes.

Napoleon had been imprisoned during the Revolution, outnumbered in Italy, stranded in Egypt, assaulted during the Brumaire coup, plotted against by Talleyrand and Fouché, opposed by no fewer than seven European coalitions, humiliated in Russia, forced to abdicate, and exiled to Elba. Yet he had come back from every reverse.

D'Erlon's corps was now beginning to regroup, and infantrymen were replacing the killed and wounded gunners of the Grand Battery. Quiot's troops were trying to force their way into La Haye Sainte. It was hardly surprising, therefore, that at 4 p.m. on Sunday, 18 June 1815, when forced to decide between retreating and trying once again to break Wellington's line before the Prussians could alter the course of the battle, Napoleon Bonaparte ordered Marshal Ney to do whatever it took to capture the walled farm that lay at the heart of the battlefield.

3

The Third Phase

THE THIRD PHASE of the battle started at 3.30 p.m., as soon as d'Erlon's bedraggled corps had stopped running and were formed back into something approaching order. Ney personally took charge of the regiments that seemed the least demoralised by their experience at the hands of the British cavalry, and led them up towards La Haye Sainte in a bid to capture the farmhouse whose possession had become as much of a talisman and a strategic necessity as was that of Hougoumont. Yet despite his best efforts, 'the bravest of the brave' initially failed to take the key point in Wellington's centre.

Meanwhile the Grand Battery and the rest of the French artillery continued pounding the Anglo-Allied lines, if anything harder than before, and despite Wellington's orders to his infantry to lie down, the cannonading caused heavy losses in the ranks. Next came a massive cavalry attack on the Anglo-Allied centre; like d'Erlon's infantry assault it was statistically one of the largest battle movements of the Napoleonic Wars.

There are a number of explanations for why the main French cavalry charge at Waterloo commenced when it did, largely unsupported by infantry as it should have been. Some historians argue that Ney mistook through his telescope the sight of some stragglers from the enemy lines who were moving back from the cannonading, as well as groups of soldiers carrying wounded comrades back to the field-hospitals, for a general withdrawal that he believed he could punish.[1] Others think that his poor performance at Quatre Bras and on the following day rankled with him to the extent that he was desperate to be seen to deliver the battle-winning stroke. Still others believe that Wellington's order to some regiments to withdraw a few paces was misinterpreted by the French.

There is certainly no written evidence to suggest that Napoleon commanded Ney to order the heavy cavalry to attack, and the Emperor later explicitly denied having done so. Ney himself was executed by firing squad that December, and his motivation was never established either. Yet in 2003 a book by the distinguished Napoleonic Wars historian Digby Smith, entitled *Charge!: Great Cavalry Charges of the Napoleonic Wars*, presented a fascinating new theory and fresh evidence about how and why the charge took place when it did, one that rings true considering the febrile mood of a cavalry regiment awaiting the order to charge. It also explains why the cuirassiers commenced their massive endeavour without the crucial infantry support that would have been so helpful.

In this explanation, based on a cock-up rather than the French historians' favoured conspiracy theories, a key figure is Captain Fortune Brack of the 2nd Guard Lancers, a relatively junior figure in a light cavalry regiment that had taken part in the destruction of Ponsonby's Union Brigade. Twenty years after the battle, Captain Brack wrote a letter to a friend (see APPENDIX II) in which he admitted personal responsibility for the disaster of Ney's premature charge. It seems that Brack, over-excited by the success against the Union Brigade, had mistaken movement on the Anglo-Allied lines for a retreat, and loudly called for an attack.

Officers around him then pushed forward to see for themselves, whereupon, as he put it: 'The right hand file of our regimental line followed them.' This movement was automatically copied along the regiment, merely in order 'to restore the alignment', but once the adjacent regiment – the Chasseurs-à-Cheval of the Guard – had also copied it, even though it was 'of only a few paces at the right', further down the line of horses it 'became more marked', so that by the time that it reached the dragoons and the Grenadiers-à-Cheval – who were impatiently awaiting the command to charge from Ney – they believed that the order had actually been given. As Brack explained: 'They set off – and we followed!'[2]

This explanation certainly takes into account the psychology of a cavalry regiment on the verge of a charge. Excitement, expectation, pumping adrenalin, keenness not to be seen as hanging back, a culture of *élan* and *esprit de corps* that prizes action over contemplation, all might have played their part. Above all it is not impossible to imagine a situation in which horses start to move forward to restore an alignment, in the process encouraging the belief that the order to charge had been given.

Whatever the true explanation – and it might even have been that Ney did not think infantry support necessary – General le Comte Milhaud's IV Cavalry Corps set off on their doomed charge towards the Anglo-Allied infantry, with Ney at their head. Seeing Milhaud's cuirassiers attack, the cavalry general Charles Lefebvre-Desnoëttes followed on without direct orders; by the time the force crossed over to the west side of the Charleroi–Brussels road it numbered forty-three squadrons of heavy cavalry, comprising about 5,000 men and horses.

It must have been an astonishing sight. As Shaw Kennedy, who watched the deployment take place, readily admitted:

The formation and advance of that magnificent and highly
disciplined cavalry had, as a spectacle, a very grand effect.
These splendid horsemen were enthusiastic in the cause of
Napoleon – full of confidence in him and in themselves –
thirsting to avenge the reverses which had been suffered
by the French armies – led by most experienced and
able cavalry commanders – and they submitted to a rigid
discipline. Their advance to the attack was splendid and
interesting in the extreme.[3]

Yet despite the formidable size of Ney's formation, Napoleon had
apparently still not seen it, and therefore did nothing to prevent
its deployment. Wellington had seen it however, and considered
it premature, and his infantry had plenty of time to take the
necessary defensive steps. Since Ney had to charge between
Hougoumont and La Haye Sainte, avoiding both as far as possible
to escape their enfilading fire, he could not ride on as broad
a front as he would have liked. When he reached the Anglo-
Allied lines he found they had altered shape. They had 'formed
square'.

Horses will refuse to charge straight at a body of men who are
pointing bayonets at them. This is the equine fact underlying the
thinking behind the defensive formation known as 'the square'.
That, and the sense of safety that the men inside squares could
take from the knowledge that their backs were protected by their
comrades. Hollow or solid, squares were actually often rectangular
or even triangular in shape, and at Waterloo several of the thirteen
or fourteen were actually oblong, but the generic title still holds.

Squares were not utterly unbreakable by cavalry, but in the
Napoleonic Wars there were only a few occasions when they had
not proved impregnable. At the battle of Garcia Hernandez in
July 1812 during the Peninsular War, two French squares were

broken by the 1st and 2nd Dragoons of the King's German Legion on a single day. The wounded horse of a trooper named Post in the latter regiment reared up and then rolled, kicking and bucking, onto the wall of Frenchmen in the front rank of the square, opening a momentary gap. This was suddenly filled with dragoons, who broke into the square.

If a square gives security because everyone's back is covered, the moment enemy cavalry get inside it the exact opposite is the case: it becomes a death-trap for infantrymen because every back is left undefended to the horsemen's sabre thrusts. The square adopted by a battalion of the French 76th Regiment of the Line at Garcia Hernandez simply collapsed, with most men surrendering, many being killed and only fifty escaping. Nor did it end there. Soon afterwards a second French square, formed by the other battalion of the 76th, also broke because its cohesion was wrecked by refugees from other parts of the battlefield trying to flood into it, just as the German dragoons fell upon it.[4]

Fortunately at Waterloo the Anglo-Allied squares had plenty of time to form up before Milhaud's cuirassiers appeared. Shaw Kennedy remarked of the attack:

> We had no idea that it would be made upon our line . . . as yet unshaken by any previous attack by infantry. The moment that it was observed that the movement of the great masses of the French heavy cavalry were directed towards his division, [Major-]General [Charles von] Alten passed the order to form oblongs, into which formation the division rapidly passed; the Guards formed squares on the right of the 3rd Division; the two divisions thus filling up the space between the Charleroi and Nivelles roads; the artillery stood in front of the infantry on the front slope of the position, so that its fire might be effectual against the attacking force.

It was indeed murderously effective, as was the entire deployment, because it allowed many muskets to be brought to bear on the cavalry, without the troops being in too much danger themselves. Squares were highly vulnerable to coordinated attack from cannon and infantry, because the square becomes a solid target of men unable to move because of the presence of cavalry. Yet Ney had launched his assault without the close support of infantry, and only six of the eleven batteries in support were the manoeuvrable horse-battery kind, further indication that the charge might have started accidentally and only been acquiesced in once it had begun. Napoleon is also quoted, whether accurately or not, as saying: 'This attack has taken place an hour too soon, but we must stand by what has already been done.'[5] Consequently the Emperor ordered General Kellermann to support Ney with his four brigades of cuirassiers and carabiniers, and also Guyot's heavy cavalry of the Guard, totalling thirty-seven squadrons to add to the forty-three already committed.

Private Charles O'Neil recorded how the British squares were 'not quite solid, but several files deep, and arranged like the squares of a chess-board; so that, if any of the enemy's cavalry should push between the divisions, they could be attacked in the rear, as well as in the front'.[6] This formation also had the advantage that the fewest number of stray shots from one square that missed the French cavalry would strike infantrymen in a nearby square. Armed with muskets whose fire was only 5 per cent accurate much beyond ten yards, this was no small advantage in an age that suffered greatly from 'friendly-fire' incidents.

The experience of being attacked by the French cavalry was something Ensign Gronow, who was serving with the 1st Foot Guards, would never forget. In his superb *Reminiscences*, he recalled being in the same square as Wellington as the enemy cavalry descended:

> You perceived at a distance what appeared to be an overwhelming, long moving line, which, ever-advancing, glittered like a stormy wave of the sea when it catches the sunlight. On came the mounted host until they got near enough, whilst the very earth seemed to vibrate under their thundering tramp. One might suppose that nothing could have resisted the shock of this terrible moving mass ... In an almost incredibly short period they were within twenty yards of us, shouting '*Vive l'Empereur!*' The word of command, 'Prepare to receive cavalry,' had been given, every man in the front rank knelt, and a wall bristling with steel, held together by steady hands, presented itself to the infuriated cuirassiers ... Our Commander-in-chief, as far as I could judge, appeared perfectly composed; but looked very thoughtful and pale.[7]

Although eighty squadrons of heavy cavalry were now ranged against the Anglo-Allied squares, Napoleon refused to send in the Imperial Guard infantry, which he always preferred to keep back until the last moment, when they had so often in the past decided battles in his favour. There was even a joke among the French line infantry that the reason the Imperial Guard were nicknamed 'the Immortals' was because they were committed so late in the day. Not only were the heavy cavalry not supported by infantry, they were not followed up by any more than six batteries of horse artillery. In the opinion of Captain Becke: 'Had guns been galloped up in the wake of the cavalry, and commenced a caseshot attack of the squares ... then nothing could have saved the centre of Wellington's line from being torn to pieces and breached.'[8]

The fact that this was not done was partly down to Napoleon, partly to Ney's over-hasty attack, but was also the result of having France's best artillerymen absent. Drouot had been taken off artillery duty to command the Guard that day, and General Desvaux, who was in command of the Guard Artillery, was killed early on in the battle, while standing close to Napoleon. (His proximity to the Emperor ought to banish the suspicions of some that Napoleon deliberately stayed entirely out of danger's way during the battle.)

The eighty squadrons comprised 10,000 horsemen, and they swiftly renewed their attack on the squares. The fighting on the plateau has been described as 'an hour of pandemonium and confused, chaotic mêlée', as every one of the squares was charged time and again. The squares took severe casualties from the horse artillery when they could find space to fire, and from mounted carabiniers and sharpshooters on foot who got close and fired their carbines at virtually point-blank range, but they also exacted a high price from the French cavalry that tried and failed to break through their close-knit ranks, bristling as they were with bayonets. Ensign Gronow recorded how he 'shall never forget the strange noises our bullets made against the breastplates of Kellermann's and Milhaud's cuirassiers . . . who attacked us with great fury'. (Although they could turn sword thrusts, breastplates were not bulletproof at short range.)

For two hours, roughly between 4 p.m. and 6 p.m., wave after wave of French heavy cavalry crashed against Wellington's infantry, but not a single square broke. Wellington himself spent the whole of the battle of Waterloo riding on his horse Copenhagen to wherever the situation was most fraught – except for Hougoumont, where he might have been trapped and unable to oversee the rest of the battle. He rode many miles that day, backwards and forwards down the line giving orders, directing batteries, looking for gaps to fill and opportunities to exploit.

It is an indication of how close Wellington came to mortal danger during the course of the battle that almost all his staff suffered death or injury. Fitzroy Somerset's left arm was actually touching Wellington's right arm when it was hit by a sharpshooter. (It later had to be amputated. 'Hallo!' Somerset cried to the surgeon, 'don't carry away that arm till I've taken off my ring.' It had been given him by Wellington's niece Emily on their wedding day.) On two occasions the Duke ran so short of aides de camp to carry messages that he had to rely on civilians, a young Swiss on one occasion and a London commercial traveller on another.[9]

During one of Ney's attacks, Wellington entered the square formed by the 73rd Regiment, part of the 3rd Division. Also inside were gunners whose cannon were in French hands outside the square, but which the French had fortuitously (and negligently) neither spiked nor towed away. As the cavalry attacks receded, these men simply ran out of the squares and resumed firing at the French, only to run back into them when the cuirassiers returned.

Not everyone followed Wellington's orders; the gallant Captain Mercer of the horse artillery disobeyed him and resolved not to command his troops to sprint into a nearby square of Brunswickers for protection. He feared that the sight of his men running might demoralise the unsteady Brunswickers, whose square he thought looked like breaking anyhow, so he ordered his men to stand firm by the guns come what may. He fired case-shot into the cavalry at only a hundred yards' range, exacting terrible carnage, and at the last moment the cavalry turned and bolted back. This was most fortunate for Mercer and his troops, since gunners caught beside their cannon by cavalry faced almost certain death.

It was during this period that Wellington was reported to have asked General Halkett, 'Well, Halkett, how do you get on?', only to receive the reply, 'My Lord, we are dreadfully cut up. Can you not relieve us for a little while?' 'Impossible,' said the Duke. 'Very well, my Lord,' answered the General stoically, 'we'll stand until the last man falls.'[10] Nor was this mere bravado, for Gronow records how:

> During the battle our squares presented a shocking sight. Inside we were nearly suffocated by the smoke and smell from burnt cartridges. It was impossible to move a yard without treading upon a wounded comrade, or upon the bodies of the dead; and the loud groans of the wounded and dying were most appalling. At four o'clock our square was a perfect hospital, being full of dead, dying and mutilated soldiers.[11]

They had two more hours of such hell to go before the cavalry attacks – some counted fourteen in all – ceased. There was some vigorous countercharging by British cavalry in protection of the squares, which inflicted significant losses on the French, albeit at a high cost.

If any part of the Anglo-Allied line, such as the Brunswickers, had indeed broken and fled the field during that part of the battle of Waterloo, it is easy to envisage a general collapse. The psychology of troops under unimaginable pressure and peril makes a fascinating study, and when panic grips a unit it can spread with astonishing speed throughout an army. At the battle of Marengo fifteen years earlier, for example, Napoleon's Armée de Réserve was hard-pressed, indeed retreating before the Austrians. His vigorous counterattack, spearheaded by Desaix, Marmont and Kellermann, suddenly created a sense of panic in the enemy after only half an hour, with the result that Marengo is considered almost as great a Napoleonic victory as Austerlitz.

Ney, now personally taking command of the last cavalry reserve of the French army, a brigade of mounted carabiniers, led one of the last charges of that part of the engagement, but this had no more success than the previous ones. Several French generals had been killed, horses were blown, casualties were tremendous, and the survivors were exhausted. On occasion the cavalry 'charges' had hardly taken place even at a trot, more like a fast walk. The last of these have been described as 'death-rides' as opposed to serious attempts to sweep the Anglo-Allied infantry off the plateau.

It is impossible to underrate the courage of the French cavalrymen who took part in these attacks, to which Gronow, as well as many others, paid honourable tribute:

> The charge of the French cavalry was gallantly executed, but our well-directed fire brought men and horses down, and ere long the utmost confusion arose in their ranks. The officers were exceedingly brave, and by their gestures and fearless bearing did all in their power to encourage their men to form again and renew their attack.[12]

What Gronow meant by 'well-directed fire' was the order to aim low, shooting at the horses rather than their riders, 'so that . . . the ground was strewed with the fallen horses and their riders, which impeded the advance of those behind them and broke the shock of the charge'. For all the tactical sense this made, Gronow did not hide the fact that 'It was pitiable to witness the agony of the poor horses, which really seemed conscious of the dangers which confronted them: we often saw a poor wounded animal raise its head, as if looking for its rider to afford him aid.'

One myth, propagated by the great French author Victor Hugo, still occasionally appears in Waterloo historiography, and needs to be dispelled. Just as when one visits Waterloo today, the way that the battle is presented might allow one to miss the fact that Napoleon lost, so the more chauvinistic French accounts sometimes claim that there was a *chemin creux d'Ohain* ('hollow way of Ohain'), or even a 'Ravine of Death', down which Ney's cavalrymen fell head-first to their and their horses' deaths. (This myth is given credence in the visually superb but historically flawed 1973 movie *Waterloo*, which starred Rod Steiger as Napoleon and Christopher Plummer as Wellington.)

In fact the hollow way, the Ohain road, was no ravine, merely an ordinary country lane slightly sunk below the level of the rest of the ground. Captain Becke in 1914 estimated that:

> At its deepest part, along Wellington's battle-line, it was merely an easy in-and-out jump, complicated by neither hedge nor ditch, either on the taking off, or on the landing side. Such an obstacle, crossed under fire, might have over-turned a few French cuirassiers as they essayed to scramble across it, it might even have loosened, or even disordered the formation of the advancing squadrons; but it could never have led to a disaster of any importance or magnitude.[13]

British cavalry brigades, such as Lord Edward Somerset's, managed to negotiate this so-called 'Ravine of Death' without ill-effect, and Shaw Kennedy, who was just above La Haye Sainte, recorded how 'the ground between them and us [the 3rd Division] presented no natural obstacles whatever'.[14] Nor were Ney, Milhaud, Dubois or any of the other generals who led the charge subsequently criticised for launching an attack into an impassable hollow or ravine. In his report to Soult, Milhaud made no mention of the ravine, and we ought to accept it as, in Thomas Carlyle's words, 'the largest ... piece of *blague* manufactured for some centuries by any man or nation'. In fact the legend of the *chemin creux* was simply created out of wounded Bonapartist pride, like so many other *ex post facto* explanations for the defeat, ranging from Bourmont's treachery, via the weather, to imperial haemorrhoids. (There is a memorial at Waterloo to Hugo, who argued that Napoleon had been defeated by God, not by the Duke of Wellington.)

By 6.30 p.m. the cavalry charges had ceased. The number of French cavalry losses has not been established. Ney's error had been to try to squeeze 10,000 cavalrymen with forty horse artillery guns into a narrow space of 1,100 yards to attack over 13,000 infantry in squares who were protected by 7,000 horsemen and seventy-five guns and howitzers. With the very difficult nature of the terrain, sucking large numbers of French cavalry into its folds and dips, in truth there was no need for an Act of God.

During Ney's cavalry assaults on the British squares, across to the east, the Prussians were advancing in force, and by 5.30 p.m. von Bülow's front two brigades (the 15th and 16th) were heavily engaged in trying to capture the château of Frischermont from General Lobau, whom Napoleon had ordered to hold up the Prussians for as long as possible while he tried to break Wellington's line. Von Gneisenau adopted a manoeuvre for arriving on the battlefield that passed the rear corps to the east through the others, which rested by the roadside. This meant that although the advance was slightly slowed when they did hit the battlefield there were no gaps in the Prussian line.

Von Bülow's entire corps numbered around 30,000 men against 10,000 under Lobau's command (of whom only 7,000 were infantry), but Lobau was a tough and resourceful general who had proved himself redoubtable in rearguard actions before, notably at the battle of Essling. His infantrymen were the 5th Line Regiment, the same men who were sent to arrest Napoleon near

Grenoble when he returned from Elba, but who had acclaimed him instead.

Sheer weight of numbers began to tell, however, as brigade after brigade issued forth out of the Bois de Paris, and Lobau was forced out of Frischermont and back to the village of Plancenoit. Later he was forced out of that too, and his force was particularly vulnerable once it was out in the open, particularly to von Bülow's plentiful infantry, cavalry and artillery. Seeing the danger of being cut off from his line of retreat, Napoleon ordered Duhesme to recapture Plancenoit with the Young Guard Division, which he managed to do by about 6.45 p.m.

The arrival of the Prussians on the battlefield in large numbers emboldened and encouraged Wellington's army as much as it demoralised Napoleon's. When at 4.30 p.m. two Prussian aides de camp passed in front of the British line in search of Wellington they were heartily cheered on their way by the Anglo-Allied soldiers. Fourteen thousand of Napoleon's reserve had to be drawn off to try to contain the Prussians, severely limiting his options and weakening his assault in the centre. As the two Prussian corps of von Pirch and von Zieten marched in from the east at about 6.30 p.m., Wellington at last saw the prospect of winning the upper hand.

Zieten's arrival on Wellington's left flank permitted a useful realignment when the 4th Brigade, commanded by Major-General Sir John Vandeleur (the 11th, 12th and 16th Light Dragoons), and the 6th Brigade under Major-General Sir Hussey Vivian (the 1st Hussars KGL, 10th and 18th Hussars), plus Sir Robert Gardiner's Horse Artillery Group, moved from the far left of the Anglo-Allied line to the centre, on von Müffling's advice. Looking through his telescope from his vantage point at Papelotte the Prussian liaison officer had seen both Zieten's proximity to Wellington's left and an ominous massing of the French infantry reserve around La Belle Alliance, presaging another huge assault on the Anglo-Allied centre and right-centre.

Vandeleur, Vivian and Gardiner arrived just in time. Captain (later Colonel) Tomkinson of the 16th Light Dragoons recalled how: 'In passing along the line it appeared to have been much cut up, and the troops, which in part held their position, were but few, and had suffered greatly. From marching under the shelter of the hill we could not distinctly see: yet I conceived from all I could learn that many points in the position were but feebly guarded.'[15] Some historians believe that without the moral and material support that Wellington was afforded by this strengthening of his centre, the fourth phase of the battle might have gone badly awry.

Meanwhile, over at Wavre, seven miles to the east of the slopes of Mont St Jean, Lieutenant-General von Thielmann was finding himself hard-pressed by Grouchy's much larger force. He sent Gneisenau a warning of defeat if he was not sent reinforcements. 'Let Thielmann defend himself as best he can,' was Gneisenau's typically blunt answer to the aide de camp who brought the message. 'It matters little if he is crushed at Wavre, so long as we gain the victory here.' Not only was Grouchy's help far too little far too late, but the Prussian high command was clear-headed enough not to allow it to draw men away from the crucial area of decision – at Waterloo.

For it was there, sometime between 6 and 6.30 p.m., that the French at last won their first concrete success, when, having completely run out of ammunition, Major Georg Baring's force finally had to evacuate the farmhouse of La Haye Sainte.

4

The Fourth Phase

ALTHOUGH THE DEFENCE of La Haye Sainte had been heroic, Major Baring's increasingly desperate requests for ammunition had not been heeded. Wellington freely admitted after the battle that it had been a terrible error not to have cut holes in the wall at the back of the farmhouse, through which extra supplies could have been passed. The farmhouse had been periodically reinforced during lulls in Ney's six-hour siege, including by the 5th Line Battalion, KGL and some 200 Nassauers, but no one seems to have done anything about the need for extra shot and powder.

Since the Germans used rifles rather than muskets, they could not be supplied with the same ammunition as the rest of the army, and there are reports of their supply wagon having been overturned on the Brussels road. Whatever the explanation, by five o'clock the situation was worrying, and by six o'clock it was desperate. Approximately 400 men of the 2nd Light Battalion, KGL, reinforced by up to 800 men later on, had held out superbly, but that could not go on indefinitely.

The French, led by Marshal Ney in person, commanding those parts of d'Erlon's corps that had not been lost or demoralised earlier in the battle, had set the roof of the farmhouse on fire. By this stage the nine companies inside La Haye Sainte only had an average of between three and four rounds of ammunition left per man. Each had started the battle with sixty rounds, which Captain Becke considered 'an inadequate amount, considering the nature of the fighting and the importance of the post'.[1] Yet the arguments made by several historians that ammunition should have been stored inside the farmhouse do not address the problem of the burning roof, and therefore the possibility of a catastrophic explosion in the courtyard.

The struggle for La Haye Sainte was described by Charles O'Neil:

> The combat now raged with unabated fury. Every inch of ground was disputed by both sides, and neither gave way until every means of resistance was exhausted. The field of battle was heaped with the dead; and yet the attacks grew more impetuous, and the resistance more obstinate.[2]

What almost all the authoritative early accounts on Waterloo and the eyewitnesses do agree upon – including Captain Becke, Henri Houssaye, Major Baring, Sir James Shaw Kennedy, Sergeant-Major Cotton, Captain Siborne, Colonel Chesney and Ney's aide Colonel Heymès – is that La Haye Sainte fell to the French sometime between 6 and 6.30 p.m. The King's German Legion were forced out of their citadel, by then collapsing in flames, at terrible cost. Of Major Baring's original 400 defenders only forty-two were still fully operational by the end of the battle, the others all being killed, wounded or captured, an appalling attrition rate. Unlike the 95th Rifles just outside the farmhouse, there had not been a single deserter.[3]

For all his shortcomings earlier on in the battle – indeed during the campaign – Marshal Ney now took speedy advantage of the fall of this strategically vital farmhouse in the centre of the battlefield, commanding the road from Charleroi to Brussels. This was the most dangerous moment in the entire battle for Wellington, affording as it did Napoleon's best opportunity to punch a hole in the Anglo-Allied centre, before the large-scale arrival of the Prussians sealed his fate.

Ney brought up horse artillery, which started to pour fire into the Anglo-Allied line at devastatingly close range. It was here that the Inniskilling Regiment took the highest casualties of any infantry unit in the army. On the battlefield today is a memorial stone commemorating the stand of the Inniskillings, and Wellington's verbal tribute to their sacrifice: 'Ah, they saved the centre of my line.'

Ney also brought forces to bear on the Sandpit, forcing out the 95th Rifle Regiment (later to become the Royal Greenjackets). According to a new history of the 95th, a hundred Riflemen were so demoralised during the course of the engagements there that they simply absented themselves without good reason for the rest of the battle.[4] An attempt to recapture the farmhouse by Colonel Ompteda and the 5th KGL was defeated, leaving Ompteda dead, the battalion virtually wiped out and the King's colours taken. The centre of the Anglo-Allied line wavered momentarily under the terrific onslaught, and this was perhaps the psychological moment at which Napoleon should have flung every available man into the action in front of the farmhouse.

That he failed to do so cannot be put down to the Emperor's lack of nerve, or lack of understanding about what was happening. His line infantry, exhausted after d'Erlon's failed efforts, were in no state to deliver the killer blow, just as his cavalry had blown itself riding in vain around the British squares. Furthermore Bülow's corps had meanwhile retaken the village of Plancenoit, less than a mile to the east of La Belle Alliance, forcing out the

Young Guard house by house and therefore threatening the whole right flank. Thus when Ney sent Colonel Heymès to beg for fresh troops to exploit the perceived weakness in Wellington's centre, Napoleon responded with heavy sarcasm: '*Des troupes! Où voulez-vous que j'en prenne? Voulez-vous que j'en fasse?*' (Troops! Where do you want me to get them from? Do you want me to make them?')

Of course the Emperor still had the bulk of the Imperial Guard to commit to the fray, but he tended only to do this at the precise moment to turn victory into a rout, which this clearly was not. Meanwhile, Wellington was in a scarcely better position, and gave repeated orders for his line to stand fast, understanding that even a modest re-alignment backwards might be misinterpreted as a withdrawal by the men themselves, which might itself turn into panic. Soldiers at the limits of their endurance, even veterans, could break and run, and Wellington – coolly riding along the line wherever he was most needed – placed cavalry regiments from his reserve directly behind infantry battalions that seemed most at risk. (When a Dutch regiment started to move back about ten yards, Wellington personally rode over to prevent it breaking and positioned the 11th Light Dragoons accordingly.)

It is astonishing that any verbal orders could be heard at all above the din of battle, a hellish wall of sound that Charles O'Neil vividly described:

> The continued reverberations of [the] pieces of artillery, the fire of the light troops, the frequent explosions of caissons blown up by shells, the hissing of balls, the clash of arms, the roar of the charges, and the shouts of the soldiery, produced a commingling of sounds whose effect it would be impossible to describe.[5]

The importance of bugle-calls, especially in cavalry charges, cannot be overstated as a means of officers communicating with their men.

If any crack in the badly damaged Anglo-Allied line had taken place, it is certain that it would have been punished badly by the French, since a large body of cuirassiers had been positioned in the dip between Hougoumont and La Haye Sainte directly the latter had fallen, out of sight of the Allied guns.

The Anglo-Allied brigades had both been very badly mauled, and the gap between General Sir Colin Halkett's right and Major-General Sir James Kempt's right was a danger area for Wellington, just as it provided Napoleon's only genuine opportunity for victory of the whole day. A strike by the Imperial Guard there at the correct psychological moment might well have broken Wellington's line and split his force in two, but even then it is doubtful that there were enough fresh French troops capable of exploiting the opportunity to the full. 'History,' wrote the great Dutch historian Pieter Geyl in his book *Napoleon: For and Against*, 'is an argument without end,' and the debate about whether Napoleon might have prevailed with a superhuman push against Wellington's centre will certainly not end soon.

Wellington was quick to recognise the danger point in his line and close it. 'I shall order the Brunswick troops to the spot, and other troops besides,' reads one of the surviving orders from this critical period to a subordinate commander. 'You go, and get all the German troops of the division to the spot that you can, and all the guns that you can find.' As Shaw Kennedy later wrote of this crucial stage:

> Of such gravity did Wellington consider this great gap in
> the very centre of his line of battle, that he not only ordered
> the Brunswick troops there, but put himself at their head:

> it was even then with the greatest difficulty that the ground could be held ... In no other part of the action was the Duke of Wellington exposed to so much personal risk as on this occasion, as he was necessarily under a close and most destructive infantry fire at a very short distance; at no other period of the day were his great qualities as a commander so strongly brought out, for it was the moment of his greatest peril as to the result of the action.[6]

Other similar last-minute arrangements saved the day in various parts of the battlefield. When Wellington sent his Acting Quartermaster-General, Major Dawson Kelly, to discover what was the meaning of the confusion he had spotted in the 30th Regiment and the 2nd Battalion of the 73rd, which had been in square formation for the greater part of the day, he received the answer that all the officers had been killed or wounded, and that Kelly would take up the command as the last French attack came up. It was repelled.

Ensign Gronow recorded how it felt to have fought throughout the afternoon, only to find that the Old Guard were being mustered for the attack:

> I am to this day astonished that any of us remained alive. From eleven o'clock till seven we were pounded with shot and shell at long and short range, were incessantly potted by *tirailleurs* [snipers] who kept up a most biting fire, constantly charged by immense masses of cavalry who seemed determined to go in and win, preceded as their visits were by a terrific fire of artillery; and, last of all, we were attacked by *la Vieille Garde* itself.[7]

The Prussians were meanwhile in the process of staving in Napoleon's right flank, even subjecting his possible future line of retreat down the Charleroi road to intense bombardment. With enemy

Above Emperor Napoleon I
(1769–1821), painted by Robert
Lefèvre. The battle of Waterloo
ended forever Napoleon's
dream of uniting Europe
under the Bonaparte dynasty.

Right Arthur Wellesley
(1769–1852), 1st Duke of
Wellington, painted by Sir
Thomas Lawrence. A supreme
tactician, Wellington's
skilful defence of the narrow
battlefield secured a decisive
Allied victory on Sunday,
18 June 1815.

Field Marshal Prince Gebhard Leberecht von Blücher (1742–1819), the Prussian commander without whose promised intervention the battle would not have been fought.

Robert Stewart (1769–1822), Viscount Castlereagh, later 1st Marquess of Londonderry, the British diplomatic genius who masterminded the strategy that finally defeated Napoleon.

A highly stylised represention of the ball thrown in Brussels by the Duchess of Richmond on 15 June 1815, which actually took place in a coachbuilder's workshop.

The battle of Quatre Bras on 16 June 1815, where the Anglo-Allied line survived French cavalry attacks.

Above A trooper and officer of
the 2nd (Royal North British)
Dragoons, better known as the
Scots Greys.

Right An officer of the 27th
(Inniskilling) Regiment, which
suffered dreadful casualties
during Waterloo.

Above An officer and trumpeter of the 6th Cuirassiers.

Right An officer of the Grenadiers of the Old Guard.

Left Count Jean-Baptiste Drouet d'Erlon (1765–184 who on either 16 (18 June might hav won the campaig for France.

Below General Sir Thomas Picton (1758–1815), who, despite being seriously wounde at Quatre Bras, led a charge at Waterloo that cost him his life.

Above Marshal Michel Ney (1769–1815), 'the bravest of the brave', who found at Waterloo that bravery was not enough.

Left Henry Paget (1768–1854), Earl of Uxbridge, later 1st Marquess of Anglesey, commander of the Anglo-Allied cavalry at Waterloo, where he lost a leg.

Above Graf August von Gneisenau (1760–1831), Blücher's chief of staff, who took the key decision after the battle of Ligny on 16 June to march north rather than east, and so made Waterloo possible.

Right General Hans von Zieten (1770–1848), commander of the Prussian 1st Corps.

Above Marquis Emmanuel de Grouchy (1766–1847), a newly created Marshal of France, who failed to march towards the sound of gunfire on the morning of Waterloo.

Left An absurdly romanticised engraving of General Pierre Cambronne (1770–1842) declining to surrender.

The British Foot Guards closing the gates at the château of Hougoumont,
where they were to hold off a vastly superior French force throughout the day.

Left Wellington's handwritten orders to the commander inside Hougoumont, instructing him what to do should the château's roof catch fire, which it did.

Below Sergeant Charles Ewart of the Scots Greys captures the eagle standard of the French 45th Regiment, which had the battle honours of Austerlitz, Jena, Friedland, Essling and Wagram emblazoned upon it.

Opposite Bonapartist historians concocted a myth that large numbers of French cavalry fell into a 'valley of death' at the sunken Ohain road, as exaggeratedly depicted here in 1910.

Left 'The Emperor will reward every man who goes through!' cried Marshal Ney towards the end of the battle, but by then breaking the Anglo-Allied line had proved impossible.

Above The Earl of Uxbridge directing sweeping-up cavalry operations towards the end of the battle.

EUGÈNE CHAPERON

Wellington meets Blücher at the fortuitously named inn, La Belle Alliance, which had been behind the French lines before the battle.

The aftermath of Waterloo, a terrible scene that prompted Wellington to remark: 'Next to a battle lost, the greatest misery is a battle gained.' He was delighted never to have to fight another.

troops at such close proximity, it is hardly surprising that the Emperor considered it of primary importance for his forces to recapture Plancenoit, a village that consequently saw as much bitter and almost equally prolonged fighting as the two more famous farmhouses of the battle, Hougoumont and La Haye Sainte.

Lieutenant-Colonel Baron Golzio was ordered to retake Plancenoit with two battalions of the 2nd Grenadier Regiment of the Old Guard, about 1,100 men, not using musketfire but only the cold steel of the bayonet. They were supported by chasseurs. Sure enough, in less than half an hour the village was cleared of fourteen battalions of Prussians, who were forced to retreat 600 yards from the village. The great obelisk to the 3,000 Prussians who died in that frenzied defence is a particularly impressive one, even on a battlefield replete with fine memorials.

While the Young Guard returned to occupy Plancenoit, the grenadiers of the Old Guard ill-advisedly pressed home their attack beyond it, even succeeding in capturing some of von Bülow's guns up a slope outside the village, but once the Prussian commander had spotted that he only faced a small detachment of the Old Guard rather than its entire strength his counterattack drove the grenadiers back into the village, which they and the Young Guard prepared to defend to the end. They had, nonetheless, bought their Emperor the one thing he needed – and the one thing that he repeatedly stated should never be lost in warfare – time.

Napoleon, having in effect won the fourth phase of battle by taking La Haye Sainte, pulverising the Anglo-Allied centre and throwing von Bülow out of Plancenoit, was now able to concentrate on trying once again to break Wellington's line. The Guard had rallied and General Lobau's VI Corps was now ready to re-engage. Five thousand men of the Guard were meanwhile fresh and ready for action. The fifth and final phase of the battle was about to begin.

5

The Fifth Phase

NAPOLEON DID NOT have much time in which to unleash the Imperial Guard onto the Anglo-Allied line, as von Zieten's column had already reached the hamlet of Smohain, thereby allowing Wellington to bring troops in from his left flank to protect his centre. Although the Prussians' advance on Napoleon's eastern flank might have been arrested, the same was not true of their forces debouching onto the battlefield further north, where they were connecting with their Anglo-Allied comrades-in-arms. The jaws of the Anglo-Prussian trap were springing shut with every new man of Blücher's army who arrived on the battlefield.

Another commander than Napoleon might have kept his eleven grenadier and chasseur battalions of the Old and Middle Guard back, in order to protect what he must have realised would be a forced retreat as the Prussians emerged onto the field en masse, but not the Emperor for whom the last two decades had been a series of gambler's lucky dice throws. The 5,000-man-strong scale of the Imperial Guard's attack would be enough, he hoped, to crack Wellington's line, which he believed must be starved of reserves by then. All he needed was to be able to exploit a crack in the line anywhere along it, and the units that had provided the *coup de grâce* so often in the past might be able to do so once again.

In preparation for his last-ditch assault Napoleon desperately needed to put heart into his troops, so he ordered his aide de camp General de la Bédoyère and other officers of his general staff to proclaim the news that Marshal de Grouchy had suddenly appeared in force on Wellington's left. According to Marshal Ney's report of the battle given to the Parisian authorities on 26 June, 'Riding along the lines, the General Officer spread this intelligence among the soldiers, whose courage and devotion remained unshaken, and they gave new proofs of them at that moment in spite of the fatigue which they experienced.' Thus heartened (if utterly mendaciously) by Napoleon, the Imperial Guard infantry marched up the slope to the east of Hougoumont to press home what they hoped would be their decisive attack. 'Audacity, further audacity, always audacity' had long been Napoleon's watchword, and it had often seen him through situations as desperate as this one.

Nor was all the news bad for the Emperor, for, as the historian Captain Becke records:

> The smoke-wreaths and puffs indicated the position with sufficient clearness. On the right, Napoleon saw Durutte in possession of Papelotte, and gradually working his way up the slope; and if the division were only strong enough to press further forward, then it would outflank the Anglo-Dutch left, and be in a position to swing down the reverse slope of the Mont St Jean plateau; whilst in the centre the remainder of d'Erlon's gallant corps crowned the ridge, beyond La Haye Sainte which was theirs at last ... In his brief survey of the historic scene Napoleon must have noticed that, in the valley away to his left, the remnants of his shattered cavalry as well as a part of Reille's Corps were rallying; and far away to the left the strife around the blazing ruins of Hougoumont still raged as furiously as

ever. Wellington's grip on his position was plainly relaxing,
whereas the Emperor still held under his hand, the Guard –
the Invincibles – whose steadiness, courage and devotion in
the past had always proved sufficient to wrest victory from
a doubtful battle.[1]

Those historians who present the attack of the Imperial Guard as
an utterly forlorn hope are therefore writing with far too much
hindsight; there had been some French successes on the battlefield
up to the point, at around 7 p.m., that Napoleon committed his
crack units to the struggle. It is nonetheless true that if Napoleon
had flung the Guard into the mêlée the moment Ney had begged
for reinforcements, they would doubtless have been able to achieve
much more.

To illustrate how 'close run' a battle Waterloo was, one only
has to consider how near the Prussian 1st Corps came to doubling
back just as it appeared on Wellington's left flank. For General
von Zieten's advance guard had suddenly halted, turned around
and returned, it transpired, upon the intelligence report of a
young and inexperienced staff officer who had misinterpreted
wounded men moving to the rear of the Anglo-Allied line as
fleeing fugitives. Blücher had ordered Zieten to close up the 1st
Corps with the main body of the Prussian army, and if it had
not been for the prompt action of General von Müffling, who
reassured Zieten that the Anglo-Allied line was holding and that
von Bülow did not need help, then Müffling's words – 'The battle
is lost if the First Corps does not go to the Duke's rescue' – might
have come hideously true. Fortunately, Zieten's mind was not as
prosaic as de Grouchy's had been, and the 1st Corps engaged,
despite the failing light.

Napoleon meanwhile gave five battalions of the Guard to Ney
for the great assault, and rode to within 600 yards of Wellington's

line to salute them as they went into battle, and to acknowledge their loyal cries of '*Vive l'Empereur!*' Another three battalions formed a second wave but did not advance beyond La Haye Sainte. Of the rest of the Guard, two battalions were installed in Plancenoit, and there were a further two at La Belle Alliance and one at Le Caillou to cover a retreat if need be. The five battalions that were about to attack – two of grenadiers and three of chasseurs – were supported by the two corps under Reille and d'Erlon, as well as cuirassiers, Guard cavalry and horse artillery.

Wellington appears to have been well apprised of the coming blow, and he certainly used the fifteen minutes before it fell in setting out his dispositions in anticipation. It seems that a deserting French cavalry officer informed the commander of the Royal Horse Artillery, Lieutenant-Colonel Augustus Frazer, where and when the attack could be expected, information that was both accurate and credible. Wellington could have expected a major attack anyhow, but the knowledge of from where it would emanate allowed him to close up his line and place the reserve cavalry brigades under Vivian and Vandeleur in the best possible positions to deal with any breakthroughs.

The Guards battalions formed three lines as they advanced up the incline. They marched with their muskets sloped upon their shoulders, almost as if they were on parade at Fontainebleau rather than taking part in the last great military manoeuvre of a hard-fought battle, indeed the last French attack of the Napoleonic Wars. The advance, with the flying flags and the sound of fife and drum, has often been described as 'unsurpassed' and 'sublime' in its initial discipline and pride. It must certainly have been an inspiring sight for a Frenchman, and a daunting one for those who stood waiting to receive its full force and fury. 'A black mass of the grenadiers of the Imperial Guard,' wrote one British observer, 'with music playing and the great Napoleon at their head, came rolling onward from the farm of la Belle Alliance.'[2]

It is worth speculating here upon the exact nature of the slope up which the Imperial Guard had to attack, for we can be nearly certain that it was not the gentle gradient that may be walked on the site of the battlefield today. After the battle a 130-foot-high mound of earth was constructed by the Dutch to commemorate the wounding of the Prince of Orange, much to the disapproval of Wellington, who when he saw it complained, 'They have ruined my battlefield.'[3] The earth for what is called the Lion Mound (after the vast stone lion atop it) was taken, it is believed, largely from the area to the north-west of it, thereby indeed wrecking the topography. Using geometric GPS satellite technology, topsoil analysis and a three-dimensional computer model, the landscape archaeologist Paul Hill has shown how there was almost certainly a relatively high ridge in 1815 that is not there today. Furthermore, there was a crop of high-standing corn that both slowed the Guard's advance and gave the Anglo-Allied forces opportunities for concealment.

It was up to this ridge that the Guard advanced in columns at about 7.30 p.m., close to one another but with enough space apart for two cannon loaded with grapeshot to be drawn up too. The first column attacked at a point roughly midway between Hougoumont and La Haye Sainte. Ney led from the van, along with Generals Friant, Roguet and Michel, and had his fifth horse of the day shot from under him. Undeterred, 'the bravest of the brave' proceeded to advance on foot. As one historian has reconstructed the scene:

> The sun was sinking, the darkened smoke-laden air made it very difficult to distinguish what was going on ... Passing their emperor with their usual tremendous salute, the

veterans hurried on, and threw themselves at Wellington's line.[4]

Waiting to receive them were more than thirty of Wellington's cannon, primed with double grapeshot. At such close range it was hard to miss ranks of men so densely packed, and the Anglo-Allied artillery on the crest of the (largely now-missing) La Haye Sainte–Hougoumont ridge ripped huge holes in the French columns. Yet still the Guard came on. The 1st battalion of the 3rd Grenadiers soon overcame a Brunswick unit and captured the guns of Major William Lloyd's Royal Artillery field brigade and Captain Cleeves' King's German Legion field brigade. They then began to engage Sir Colin Halkett's brigade, pressing back the already badly-mauled 30th and 73rd Regiments.

The advance of the 3rd Grenadiers was halted, and eventually reversed, partly by the speed and courage of a Dutch brigade under General Baron David de Chassé, which Wellington had recalled from Braine l'Alleud as soon as he had recognised that Napoleon did not intend to mount any attacks beyond the Nivelles road on his right flank. Chassé deployed a Dutch-Belgian horse battery that volleyed grapeshot into the Guard, and then sent in 3,000 Dutch-Belgian infantry whose bayonets turned the grenadiers back down the slope. Never should the non-British and non-Prussian contribution to the victory be underestimated, since the repulse of the elite 1st/3rd Grenadiers of the Guard – a moment as important psychologically as it was tactically – was largely accomplished by these Dutch-Belgian troops. Just as it is an absurd question to ask whether Wellington could have won Waterloo without Blücher – because he would have never fought the battle – so it is equally pointless to consider a battle fought without the Dutch and Belgian contingents.

While Chassé was engaging the 3rd Grenadiers, the 4th Grenadiers of the Guard, reduced to a single battalion by its losses at Ligny two days earlier, attacked the right flank of Sir Colin Halkett's brigade, supported by two guns of the Guard horse artillery reserve. The combined musket and grapeshot fire caused the British 33rd and 69th Regiments to waver, but any thought of retreat was banished by Halkett himself waving the flag of the 33rd above his head. Both regiments stood firm and the 4th Grenadiers were eventually also repulsed. Wellington's centre had withstood the attack of the first Guard echelon, the grenadiers. Now was the time for the second and third echelons, made up of chasseurs.

Marching in two columns through and over the human and horseflesh debris of Ney's futile cavalry attacks earlier in the day – 'The ground was completely covered with those brave men, who lay in various positions, mutilated in every conceivable way'[5] – the three battalions of chasseurs also almost reached the crest of Wellington's (today non-existent) ridge. They had been subjected to roundshot fire from the horse artillery troop formerly commanded by Major Norman Ramsay (who had been killed earlier in the day) from the moment they had formed up thousands of yards back near La Belle Alliance, but by the time they reached their destination their ammunition was getting scarce. Certainly the roared war-cries of the chasseurs could be easily heard over the boom of the cannon. Yet their formation was effectively split by the nature of the ridge, which is very apparent if one stands to the south of La Haye Sainte and advances north-north-west; visitors to the battlefield are encouraged to do this in order to appreciate the difficulties the Guard had in trying to stay together in this great assault.

As the 1st and 3rd Chasseurs à Pied of the Middle Guard

mounted the crest in their attempt to reach the Ohain road – in some places they were only about twenty yards off – they were suddenly faced by the apparition of the British 1st Foot Guards rising up from out of the corn where Wellington had hidden them. 'Up Guards, ready!' is one of the many versions of the command that the Duke gave them as they presented their muskets and volleyed at almost point-blank range. Lieutenant Captain Harry Weyland Powell of the 1st Regiment of Foot Guards described the scene:

> Whether it was from the sudden and unexpected appearance of a Corps so near them, which must have seemed as starting out of the ground, or the tremendously heavy fire we threw into them, *La Garde*, who had never before failed in an attack, suddenly stopped. Those from a distance and more who could see the affair, tell us that the effect of our fire seemed to force the head of the column bodily back.[6]

Meanwhile, field brigades such as that of Captain Napier fired grapeshot at ranges of 200 yards and less, and the troops of the 3rd Chasseurs who still wanted to close with the enemy found that they had to climb over the corpses of their fallen comrades in order to do so. The assault petered out. Superb inter-service coordination between the British infantry and artillery had been the key to the repulse of the 3rd Chasseurs.

After ten minutes or so of further carnage, Wellington sensed the correct moment to order the Foot Guards to fix their bayonets and charge, whereupon the 3rd Chasseurs were chased off the slopes and back to Hougoumont and beyond. Ensign Gronow took part in this engagement, recalling how:

> We rushed on with fixed bayonets and that hearty 'hurrah' peculiar to British soldiers. It appeared that our men, delib-

erately and with calculation, singled out their victims, for as they came upon the Imperial Guard our line broke, and the fighting became irregular. The impetuosity of our men seemed almost to paralyse their enemies: I witnessed several of the Imperial Guard who were run through the body apparently without any resistance on their parts. I observed a big Welshman of the name of Hughes, who was six feet seven inches in height, run through with his bayonet and knock down with the butt-end of his firelock, I should think a dozen at least of his opponents.[7]

So many British troops followed them down that Napier's battery was forced to stop firing altogether. Soon they had to break off their pursuit and turn back, however, because the last battalion of the Middle Guard, the 4th Chasseurs, could now be seen advancing towards the battered but still unbroken Anglo-Allied line. This truly was Napoleon's last throw.

Facing the veterans of the Middle Guard were a hodgepodge of Anglo-Allied units. Some – like Major-General Frederick Adam's brigade on the left flank of the enemy – were fresh, although others – such as Halkett's brigade and the Foot Guards – were badly depleted. To complete the Middle Guard's sense of utter isolation, the 3rd Hanoverian brigade actually debouched from Hougoumont and started to fire into their rear. It was Colonel Sir John Colborne who dealt the Middle Guard its final *coup de grâce* when he brought up his battalion of the 52nd Light Infantry to its left flank and fired a withering volley into the French ranks. Once the rest of Adam's brigade had followed this up with a bayonet charge, the Guard broke and ran.

Wellington once again sensed the ideal moment. He snapped his telescope shut, rode to the crest of the ridge, took off his hat and waved it to indicate a general advance across the entire battlefront to mop up any further resistance. The exact words he used at that moment are disputed, but are often quoted as: 'Go forward, boys, and secure your victory.'

The cavalry brigades of Vivian and Vandeleur which Wellington had hitherto used sparingly – Vandeleur to extricate the Union Brigade, for example – were also then finally unleashed to break through any places where the French might attempt to stand and resist. Sir Augustus Frazer recalled two days later what it had been like fighting in the dwindling twilight:

> I have seen nothing like that moment, the sky literally dark-ened with smoke, the sun just going down, and which till then had not for some hours broken through the gloom of a dull day, the indescribable shouts of thousands, where it was impossible to distinguish between friend and foe. Every man's arm seemed to be raised against that of every other. Suddenly, after the mingled mass had ebbed and flowed, the enemy began to yield, and cheerings and English huzzas announced that the day must be ours.[8]

It was at around 8 p.m. that the cry went up through the French ranks, '*La Garde recule!*', something that had never happened before in the eleven-year history of the *crème de la crème* of the Grande Armée. It could mean only one thing: that the battle was irretrievably lost, and the only option now left was to throw down one's musket and flee. The cry '*Sauve qui peut!*' quickly re-placed '*La Garde recule!*', as the French army disintegrated before Napoleon's eyes.

The Emperor bravely attempted to rescue the situation at La Haye Sainte by ordering the three Guards units still under his control – the second battalions of the 1st Chasseurs, 2nd Chasseurs and 2nd Grenadiers, under Generals Cambronne, Christiani and Roguet – to form three squares a hundred yards from the farmhouse, with their right almost reaching the Charleroi road. These initially withstood Vivian's hussars, but then had to contend with both British infantry musketry and the horrific grapeshot fire of both Brevet-Major Whinyates' and Lieutenant-Colonel Gardiner's horse artillery troops and a field brigade under Brevet-Major Rogers, all firing at only about sixty yards' range.

Almost impregnable to cavalry, squares are nonetheless highly vulnerable to infantry and artillery due to their highly compact nature and the paucity of muskets that can be brought to bear on any one spot, and so the carnage was terrific. After dreadful punishment, the Guard were ordered to fall back to La Belle Alliance by the Emperor, who rode off with some mounted chasseurs to try to find another position from which to rally his stricken forces, deciding upon Genappe.

It was during the Guards' retreat that General Cambronne was asked whether he would surrender, to which he reputedly merely answered: '*Merde!*' A myth was soon created that he had in fact replied: '*La Garde meurt, elle ne se rend pas.*' ('The Guard dies, it does not surrender.') By the time the units reached La Belle Alliance their hitherto admirable order had collapsed. At this point, the Guard neither died nor surrendered; it simply ran, just like the rest of Napoleon's army.

Lobau's troops managed to protect the fleeing Armée du Nord as it swarmed back down the Charleroi road, whence it had come in such high expectations the previous day. The track itself was torn up by the ceaseless pounding of Prussian roundshot, fired from the by now re-recaptured village of Plancenoit (where General Duhesme was killed). Meanwhile the Prussian cavalry gave murderous chase, taking every advantage to revenge themselves on the men who had devastated their Fatherland nine years before during the Jena campaign.

Frenchmen were being lanced in the back by Prussian cavalry for as long as there was still daylight enough for the uhlans to carry out their long-awaited work of retribution. Their methodical vengeance helped turn a devastating and decisive defeat for France into an utter rout. Sergeant-Major Cotton of the 7th Hussars recorded: 'That the French in their flight from Waterloo were unnecessarily butchered during many hours by the exasperated Prussians, is a fact, which I can more easily explain than justify.'[9]

In the course of the rout some terrible things happened on the Allied side, too, as when Captain Mercer's horse artillery battery came under heavy enfilading 'friendly' fire from a Prussian battery, forcing Mercer to break off his pursuit of the French; the bombardment disabled his guns and killed no fewer than 140 of his 200 horses.

Crying, 'Come and see a Marshal of France die!', Ney put himself at the head of a brigade which by then consisted of only two battalions. It was not too tempting an offer for a unit that belonged to Durutte's division of d'Erlon's corps, and so which had therefore seen plenty of fighting already, and the counter-attack that Ney led soon petered out. As he explained to Joseph Fouché on 26 June: 'As for myself, constantly with the rearguard which I followed on foot, having had all my horses killed under me, being worn out with fatigue, covered with contusions, and having no longer the strength to march, I owed my life to a corporal, who supported me on the road.'

Napoleon himself, escorted by a small staff and even smaller bodyguard, got back to Le Caillou, where he discovered the 1st Battalion of the 1st Chasseurs of the Guard, which accompanied him on the road back to Charleroi and eventually to Paris.

One month after Waterloo, Napoleon surrendered to the Royal

Navy man-of-war HMS *Bellerophon*, and was transported first to Plymouth and then to exile on St Helena, where he remained for the almost six years that remained to him before his death in May 1821.

As the good luck of a dedicated journal-keeper would have it, Ensign Gronow was present at La Belle Alliance, the inn that had been behind Napoleon's lines at the start of the battle, when Blücher met Wellington there at 9 p.m. 'The Duke of Wellington, who had given rendezvous to Blücher at this spot, then rode up, and the two victorious generals shook hands in the most cordial and friendly manner,' he recorded.[10] Speaking the only language both understood, that of their defeated foe, Blücher said to Wellington: '*Quelle affaire!*', which might colloquially be translated as 'What a business!', or – even more colloquially – 'Wow!' With that superbly understated punchline, the 'long' eighteenth century could finally be brought to a close.

CONCLUSION

THE WATERLOO CAMPAIGN, like almost any military engagement, was compounded of strategic and tactical errors on both sides, including serious communications and intelligence blunders, tragic friendly-fire incidents, and occasionally an indictable lack of initiative. Few but the Emperor's most chauvinistic acolytes will deny that many more mistakes, both in quantity and gravity, were made by the French side than by the Anglo-Allied-Prussian coalition.

Wellington, it is true, was caught largely unawares by Napoleon's incredibly swift deployment of the Armée du Nord. He was, by his own admission, 'humbugged'. It is on balance unfair to criticise Wellington for leaving his army too widely dispersed before Napoleon attacked, since he had a huge area of operations to patrol and did not know where that attack might fall – or even if Brussels, rather than, say, the Channel ports was in fact the Emperor's prime objective. (He also had a duty to protect Louis XVIII's exiled court in Ghent.)

Yet Wellington's immediate troop dispersals after he had coherent and trustworthy word that Napoleon was on the offensive have been very severely criticised, particularly in recent works by the historian Peter Hofschröer. It is also undeniable that in a despatch written at 10.30 a.m. on 16 June – the day of Ligny and Quatre Bras – Wellington misled Blücher about the exact position of some of his troops. Other historians such as Jac Weller and

John Ropes argue that this was unintentional and the result of the 'muddle' of Wellington's Quartermaster-General Colonel Sir William De Lancey, whose papers were subsequently lost after he was mortally wounded at Waterloo.[1] It is difficult to accept that Wellington misled his ally on purpose, but this debate will doubtless continue. Nor is the blame all one-sided: the intelligence that Gneisenau and Zieten gave Wellington has been described by one distinguished historian of the campaign as 'incomplete and late'.[2]

The criticism made of Wellington that at such a crucial moment as the evening of 15 June he went to the Duchess of Richmond's ball is more easily dealt with. By attending – if only relatively briefly – he calmed the fears of the Brussels populace, put heart into his assembled colonels, showed that Sir Francis Drake was not the only British hero to display insouciance in the face of danger, and lost little by it, since not much serious fighting – perhaps 3,000 casualties incurred by the French and the Prussians – had taken place that day.

The accusation that Wellington left too many troops at Hal, covering an attack from Napoleon that never transpired, does not fully take into account Napoleon's track record, something that Wellington took great pains never to underestimate. Among several other French historians, General Jomini argued that Napoleon should indeed have chosen the more open route to Brussels via Mons, employing wide circling movements on the extreme left flank, not least to avoid the bottleneck before the Forest of Soignes. By the time it was clear that Napoleon had no extra troops to effect this it was far too late to bring the Hal detachment over to Waterloo, even supposing that Wellington had not intended them to help cover his retreat to Ostend were he defeated.[3] It was an error of Napoleon's – one attested to by Soult,

Reille, Foy and indeed Wellington himself – to have adopted the frontal assault tactic at Waterloo, but, crucially, it was not one that Wellington could have known was going to be made. Hence, Hal was an acceptable insurance policy.

Both General Picton and Napoleon criticised Wellington's choice of battlefield at Waterloo, but few have agreed with them. The folds in the ground, the east–west lateral Ohain road hidden from enemy view, the advanced farmhouses and flanking woodland made the battlefield ideal for the kind of dogged infantry and artillery defensive action that the British army excelled at and in which Wellington was expert. A visit to the battlefield itself – which I very heartily recommend to any reader of this book – will, especially if one has the energy to climb the Lion Mound, immediately allow one to appreciate its advantages to the defender. (It should be recalled that Picton only saw one part of the battlefield, and died before he had a chance to appreciate the rest, and that Napoleon had his own bitter and political personal reasons for criticising Wellington's displacements.)

The loss of La Haye Sainte has also been put down to Wellington's not supervising the resupply of ammunition to Baring's 2nd Light Battalion of the King's German Legion, who fought with rifles rather than standard-issue muskets and therefore needed specialised powder and shot. The wagon that carried the battalion's ammunition had overturned in a ditch, but it was surely up to Baring rather than the commander-in-chief to see to its rescue.

By contrast with these relatively footling complaints, the errors made by Napoleon and other French commanders during the Waterloo campaign were severe, indeed perhaps even decisive. The first blunder might simply have been for Napoleon to have quitted Elba at all, considering the unanimity of European opinion about his unfitness for the throne and therefore the inevitable invasions of France that it would trigger. Yet his own destiny was always more important to Napoleon than the thousands – and finally millions – of lives that were lost in the course of his pursuit of it.

The Emperor's next error, at least so Wellington believed, was to have struck north and fought on coalition territory rather than fighting defensively inside France. Some of Napoleon's best victories had been won with relatively small forces in 1814, and the border fortresses of France could have held up large numbers of coalition soldiers for months. Instead Napoleon was impelled by the political advantages he felt would accrue from a restoration of *la Gloire* and a magnificent entry into Brussels.

Although Ney has been criticised for not capturing Quatre Bras early on 16 June, there is some debate about exactly when Napoleon actually ordered him to do so. This has been greatly complicated by the ex-Emperor's almost complete inability when in exile on St Helena to tell the truth about anything much regarding the campaign.[4] His zeal in laying the entire blame for his defeat on Ney, d'Erlon, Grouchy and several others – none of whom was admittedly guiltless – led him to play very fast and loose with the facts. Over Quatre Bras, for example, he claimed that he had ordered Ney to capture the crossroads at dawn, whereas twenty years later Ney's son published the actual orders which showed that of the three instructions Ney received, the first did not mention Quatre Bras and the one that did was written several miles away, at Fleurus, at about 10 a.m. Indeed, Weller goes so far as to state of Ney: 'That he began his battle as soon as he did is probably to his credit.'[5]

Whoever was to blame for the fact that General d'Erlon's corps arrived at neither the battlefield of Quatre Bras nor at Ligny on

16 June, at either of which it could have been decisive, must bear heavy responsibility for the loss of the campaign. History has still not precisely ascertained the guilty party. The fact that d'Erlon spent six hours marching between battlefields cannot wholly be put down to the General himself, who had little option but to obey the commands of the Emperor, Marshal Ney, or Marshal Soult, the chief of staff, but a little more initiative from him when he was within striking distance of either Ligny or Quatre Bras would have paid dividends. If Nelson could affect a blind eye to a signal, d'Erlon might just as easily have disobeyed the command to trek back across country until 9.30 p.m. without ever firing a shot in anger.

Napoleon certainly missed two important opportunities on Saturday, 17 June, in simultaneously allowing Wellington to retreat from Quatre Bras and in losing all connection with the Prussians as they escaped northwards to Wavre. Grouchy should probably not have been sent off to follow the Prussians at all, but if he was going to be, he needed to be despatched at daybreak, not in the afternoon, by which time the trail had gone cold.[6] 'March together! Strike together!' was a favourite military maxim of Napoleon's; another was 'An enemy should be outflanked, or enveloped, without separating one's own force.'[7] These sensible rules of warfare were emphatically not adhered to by their author during Saturday, 17 and Sunday, 18 June 1815.

At Waterloo the French ought to have attacked Wellington's position the moment that all their troops had arrived from Rosomme, breakfasted and cleaned their weapons after the previous night's downpour. It is very doubtful that that cold, windless and largely sunless Sunday morning really dried the ground to any great degree for the artillery. Once again, it was simply time wasted.[8]

When battle was joined before noon, and the Grand Battery's eighty-four guns had opened up on the Anglo-Allied position, Grouchy ought to have immediately marched westwards towards the sound of them, as his subordinate General Gérard urged. Yet this would have been to disobey Napoleon's direct orders, sent at only ten o'clock that morning, to march on Wavre. It is also unlikely that even if Grouchy had taken Gérard's advice and marched towards Plancenoit he would have got there in time to affect the outcome of the battle, because he would have soon encountered the Prussian divisions of Pirch and Thielmann, which would have held up his advance, while those of Bülow and Zieten could have carried on to help Wellington.[9]

On the battlefield itself, the French failure to use any artillery to batter and breach the walls of Hougoumont was a palpable error, as was the perhaps unimaginative divisional formation adopted by d'Erlon's corps in its attack on the Anglo-Allied line. Napoleon and Ney's decisions to attack with infantry under-supported by cavalry and artillery, and later with cavalry under-supported by infantry and artillery, must also be regarded – for whatever tactical reason they were made – as grave errors. (Equally, Uxbridge was gravely at fault for allowing his cavalry counterattack against d'Erlon so disastrously to overreach itself.)

The timing of Ney's great cavalry charge is similarly open to criticism, as taking place too early and going on for too long after it had failed in its objective to overwhelm the Anglo-Allied infantry, which had formed into squares. If, as seems to be the case from the new evidence presented in Appendix II, the charge happened largely by accident, this cannot really be laid at Napoleon's door. By the time the Imperial Guard was committed towards the end of the battle, Napoleon cannot be blamed for rashness; there was virtually no other choice for him at that stage.

The Guard was well-supported, but it still adopted a columnar formation that the British Peninsular infantry had turned back again and again over six years of continuous campaigning.

It is easy enough to enumerate the errors made on both sides during the Waterloo campaign, yet the difficulties that the commanders were acting under ought to be recalled. Communications could go no faster than a man on horseback, and by the time messages arrived they could be out of date. Commanders could see no further than topography and telescopes allowed them – indeed one of Wellington's wisest sayings was: 'All the business of war, and indeed all the business of life, is to endeavour to find out what you don't know by what you do; that's what I call "guessing what was at the other side of the hill".' Sometimes commanders even had to guess what was directly in front of them, since the huge quantities of thick smoke emanating from the constant firing of cannon and muskets could wreathe and envelop a battlefield, cloaking large areas in dense, impenetrable grey. Thus snap decisions had to be taken from sudden and partial glimpses of the scene.

It is important not to employ too much hindsight in retelling the battle of Waterloo, since otherwise it might seem simply like a catalogue of errors on both sides, the victory going to the one that made the fewest. In fact Napoleon's preference for mass frontal assault rather than manoeuvre did make Wellington's job easier, but however sturdy the Anglo-Allied infantry were en masse there were also desertions, even – as in the case of the Cumberland Hussars – of an entire regiment.

The French outnumbered their opponents at the opening of the battle, especially in artillery; they had been victorious two days earlier; they were a homogeneous national force; and their morale was high owing to their being commanded in person by a general they firmly believed to be the greatest soldier since Alexander. The battle was therefore by no means a foregone conclusion, especially when La Haye Sainte fell at around 6.15 p.m. Wellington was right when he opined that Waterloo had been 'a damned nice thing – the nearest run thing you ever saw in your life ... By God, I don't think it would have done if I had not been there.'

Nearly 71,000 men were killed or wounded in the battle of Waterloo and its immediate aftermath, to which horrific toll must be added 2,600 casualties in frontier clashes on 15 June, the 32,500 at Ligny, 8,800 at Quatre Bras, 400 on the retreat from Quatre Bras and 5,000 at Wavre – making a total of 120,300. Nationally, the breakdown over the entire 15–18 June period was roughly as follows: French casualties 67,500; Prussian 30,000; and Anglo-Allied 22,800. Sergeant-Major Cotton recalled: 'The field of battle, after the victory, presented a frightful and most distressing spectacle. It appeared as if the whole military world had been collected together, and that something beyond human strength and ingenuity had been employed to cause its destruction.'[10] Charles O'Neil wrote that 'the groans of the wounded and the shrieks of the dying were heard on every side'. The pillaging of the corpses by local Belgian peasants, who, it was widely reported, were not above slitting the throats of the wounded the more easily to rifle their pockets, was a ghastly reality of the aftermath of the battle. O'Neil recorded how the morning after the battle 'the mangled and lifeless bodies were, even then, stripped of every covering – everything of the smallest value was already carried off'.[11] As Wellington himself remarked: 'Next to a battle lost, the greatest misery is a battle gained.'

'Every man meets his Waterloo at last,' wrote the nineteenth-century American moralist Wendell Phillips, and the phrase has indeed slipped into the English language to imply that there is a fate, an inescapable destiny, awaiting us all. Yet was this really the case for that ultimate Man of Destiny, Napoleon Bonaparte? His career had hitherto been a series of floutings of the supposedly immutable laws of Providence. Like that of the great Mithridates Eupator, King of Pontus a century before Christ, Napoleon's life had been a tale of unlikely adventures that each seemed to herald disaster but which time and again were turned into victories.

Just as Mithradates eventually met his Panticapæum, so Napoleon met his Waterloo. Even had Napoleon won there he would sooner or later have been defeated by one or more of the vast Russian, Austrian and Prussian armies that were converging upon France. So does that mean that Waterloo was in fact insignificant, not one of the great turning points of history at all? No; it is important because of the decisive and undeniable way that it finished off *la Gloire*, the French sense of military superiority that had been the central factor of European politics ever since Napoleon had taken over command of the Army of Italy in March 1796. Without *la Gloire*, France has had to live on her myths and with her ever-mounting roll of defeats, from Sedan to 1940 to Dien Bien Phu.

If it opened a long era of French military humiliation, Waterloo also heralded the true beginning of the modern British Empire. Of course there had been significant colonial acquisitions long before Waterloo, including the Indian, Canadian and Caribbean territories won in the Seven Years' War in the mid-eighteenth century, but the victory at Waterloo and the subsequent Congress of Vienna set Britain on the path of seemingly unlimited imperial territorial acquisition. With crucial nodal points being awarded to the United Kingdom by the Final Act of the Congress of Vienna, such as Malta, Heligoland, Ceylon, Tobago and Santa Lucia, as well as the sale of the Cape Colonies to Britain by Holland, Britain had all the strategic building blocks in place necessary for her subjects to swarm over Africa and Asia in the way they were to do over the next century.

The United States, too, benefited – if at one remove – from the defeat of Napoleon, following which there was not even the faintest danger of the Louisiana Purchase of 1804 being renationalised by a powerful French Empire. After the end of her two wars against Britain between 1812 and 1815, the United States was left entirely free to expand westwards and devote all her energies into exploiting her apparently limitless continental resources. By 1900 she could plausibly claim to have a manifest destiny to become a global superpower, which she triumphantly did in the coming twentieth century.

APPENDIX I

Major Robert Dick's Letter from Brussels

The writer of this hitherto unpublished letter was Robert Henry Dick, son of Dr William Dick of Tullymeet House, Perthshire. At the time of writing Robert Dick was a major in the 42nd Royal Highland Regiment (the Black Watch), although with the brevet rank of lieutenant-colonel since October 1812. He had fought at the battles of Fuentes d'Onoro and Salamanca. Unlike most letters about Waterloo, which were sent after the battle, this was written prior to it. It is in the possession of the author.

We know that Dick attended the Duchess of Richmond's ball on 15 June 1815 because 'Col. Dick, 42nd (killed at Sobraon, 1846)' appears in the list of attendees that Lady de Ros gave to Sir William Fraser, and his name can be found on page 27 of Sir William's 1897 account of the occasion, *The Waterloo Ball*.

The morning after the ball the 42nd were rushed to the battle-field of Quatre Bras as part of the 5th Division, arriving there just before 3 p.m. on 16 June. In the fierce fighting Sir Robert Macara, a colonel of the regiment, was killed, and Robert Dick – who had been seriously wounded by a musket shot to the shoulder – took over command until he fainted from loss of blood. The regiment finally withdrew as evening fell, and fought against d'Erlon's corps at Waterloo two days later. Dick rose to command the 73rd Regiment in 1845, only to die at the moment of victory at the battle of Sobraon the following year.

This letter, sent to his father in set H4 at Albany, in Piccadilly, is evocative of the atmosphere in the upper reaches of the British army less than a week before Waterloo:

Brussels. June 12th 1815
My Very Dear Father
I was in hopes ere this to have had the pleasure of hearing from you in answer to the letter I wrote you from this place on my arrival. Our Division has been formed here consisting of two British brigades and one Hanoverian. We have been pretty much employed our Regiment being very fond of giving as little trouble as possible. The Duke [of Wellington] gave another Ball the other night and when he saw me came up again and shook hands. The Duchess of Richmond who was there a little time after which I was speaking asked me if I had heard of the Marquis [of Huntly, the Duchess's brother, and a colonel in the 42nd]. I said not but was anxious to see him as I wished him to interest himself to get me the 2nd colonelcy of the Regiment. She said she was sure her brother would do anything he could for me and then turning round said; that Great Man pointing to the Duke would I am sure do so likewise for I never heard him speak more handsomely of any young man than he did of you last night at my house. It may not be of any service but at any rate it is pleasant to be spoken well of by so great a Man. I have been invited to the Duchess's parties and am engaged to one on Thursday next. If we remain but from what I hear from very good authority I think that the army will move away soon. I hope we shall make a good hand of it, but I wish we had the Army the Duke had in Spain. The British Infantry is in five Divisions (another division is forming at Ghent) consisting in Effectives not more than four thousand R & I in each Division. The Cavalry British seven thousand very fine & there is a great force of Artillery. I suppose the whole British cannot be much more than thirty five thousand Effectives. There are 29 thousand

Belgians, not I fear to be trusted as they all have served under Bone [Bonaparte]. The Dutch are about 30 thousand. I am told pretty good [but] I have not seen them. The Hanoverians are fine both Cavalry and Infantry. Each British division has a brigade of them. It is said Soult has arrived to take the Command of the Army. Approved by Wellington. A Blow will be struck by one side or other before the 23rd of this month. I am astonished Bone does not attack either Prussians or us before the whole of the Russians arrive. He might beat us in detach. I have not seen [his brother-in-law Lieutenant-Colonel the Hon. William George] Harris [who was to command the 2nd Battalion of the 73rd Regiment at Waterloo] as yet. I have been intending to go every day but something or other has always prevented me. My Horses have lamed one another & are hardly able to move & one I was obliged to shoot yesterday for the Flanders malady. I had him in a different stable from the others or I should have lost all of them and have been ruined. I heard from Harris yesterday he was quite well.

I am ever

Your Dutiful Son

R. H. D.

Captain Fortune Brack's Letter of 1835

This is taken from the letter written twenty years after the battle by Captain Fortune Brack of the 2nd Chevaux-légers Lancers of the Guard, who might well have been instrumental in catapulting Ney's cavalry towards its disastrous series of attacks against the British squares. It was originally quoted in Digby Smith's *Charge!: Great Cavalry Charges of the Napoleonic Wars* (Greenhill Books) in 2003. Considering what catastrophe sprang from Captain Brack's actions, it is unlikely that he would have wished to invent his testimony. Certainly, one may search in vain for the name of Captain Brack in books on Waterloo. In my view Mr Smith has made a significant contribution to the sum of our knowledge of why, ultimately, Napoleon fell from power. Here is Brack's explanation, which is worth reprinting at length not only for its intrinsic evidence, but also for the superb description of what it was like for a lancer to charge a square:

> Impassioned by our recent success against Ponsonby, and by the forward movement that I had noticed being executed by the cuirassiers on our right, I exclaimed, 'The English are lost! The position on which they have been thrown back makes it clear. They can only retreat by one narrow road confined between impassable woods. One broken stone on this road and their entire army will be ours! Either their general is the most ignorant of officers, or he has lost his

head! The English will realise their situation – there – look
– they have uncoupled their guns.'

I was ignorant of the fact that the English batteries usually
fought uncoupled.

I spoke loudly, and my words were overheard. From the
front of our regiment a few officers pushed forward to join
our group. The right hand file of our regimental line followed them; the movement was copied in the squadrons to
the left to restore the alignment, and then by the Chasseurs-
à-Cheval of the Guard. This movement, of only a few paces
at the right, became more marked [as it was copied] to the
left. The brigade of the Dragoons and the Grenadiers-à-
Cheval, who were awaiting the order to charge at any
moment, believed this had been given.

They set off – and we followed!

That is how the charge of the Imperial Cavalry took place,
over the reason for which so many writers have argued so
variously.

From that moment, lining up to the left, we crossed the
[Charleroi–Brussels] road diagonally so as to have the whole
Guard cavalry on the left side of this road. We crossed the
flat ground, climbed up the slope of the plateau upon which
the English army was drawn up, and attacked together.

The order in which that army was drawn up, or the part
exposed to our view, was as follows:

To the right were the Scots Foot, close to the undergrowth
which extended to the bottom of the slope. This infantry
delivered heavy and well-directed fire.

Then came the squares of line infantry, ordered in a
chequerboard pattern, then similar squares of Hanoverian
Light infantry; then a fortified farm [La Haye Sainte].

Between the squares were uncoupled batteries, whose
gunners were firing and then hiding under their guns,
behind them some infantry and some cavalry.

We were nearly level with this farm, between which
and us our cuirassiers were charging. We rode through

the batteries, which we were unable to drag back with us.

We turned back and threatened the squares, which put up a most honourable resistance.

Some of them had such coolness, that they were still firing ordered volleys by rank.

It has been said that the Dragoons and Grenadiers-à-Cheval to our left broke several squares, personally I did not see it – and I can state that we Lancers did not have the same luck, and that we crossed our lances with the English bayonets in vain. Many of our troopers threw their weapons like spears into the front ranks to try to open up the squares.

The expenditure of ammunition by the English front line and the compact pattern of the squares which composed it meant that the firing was at point-blank range, but it was the harm which the artillery and the squares in the second line were doing to us, in the absence of infantry and artillery to support our attack, which determined our retreat.

We moved slowly and faced front once again in our position at the bottom of the slope, so that we could just make out the English front line.

It was then that Marshal Ney, alone and without a single member of his staff accompanying him, rode along our front and harangued us, calling out to the officers he knew by their names. His face was distracted, and he called out again and again, 'Frenchmen, let us stand firm! It is here that the keys to our freedom are lying!' I quote him word for word.

Five times we repeated the charge; but since the conditions remained unchanged, we returned to our position at the rear five times.

The Duke of Wellington's
Waterloo Despatch

Wellington's despatch reporting the battle of Waterloo was written on the following day, and published in *The Times* and the *London Gazette Extraordinary* on Thursday, 22 June 1815. It is a masterpiece of concise Wellingtonian prose, if not always entirely factually accurate in every regard, since the Duke was writing immediately after the events and only heard about some aspects of the battle from others.

The despatch was sent as a letter to Earl Bathurst, the Secretary for War, and summed up all the actions that had taken place since the start of the campaign; here is an edited version, retaining Wellington's spelling and grammar:

> Waterloo, June 19, 1815
> My Lord,
> Buonaparte having collected the 1st, 2nd, 3rd, 4th, and 6th corps of the French army and the Imperial Guards, and nearly all the cavalry on the Sambre, and between that river and the Meuse, between the 10th and the 14th of the month, advanced on the 15th and attacked the Prussian posts at Thuin and Lobez, on the Sambre, at day light in the morning.
> I did not hear of these events till the evening of the 15th, and immediately ordered the troops to prepare to march, and afterwards to march to their left, as soon as I had intelligence from other quarters to prove that the

enemy's movement upon Charleroy was the real attack . . .

[Of the battles of Ligny and Quatre Bras:] The Prussian army maintained their position with their usual gallantry and perseverance, against a great disparity of numbers, as the 4th corps of their army, under General Bulow, had not joined, and I was not able to assist them as I wished, as I was attacked myself, and the troops, the cavalry in particular, which had a long distance to march, had not arrived.

We maintained our position also, and completely defeated and repulsed all the enemy's attempts to get possession of it. The enemy repeatedly attacked us with a large body of cavalry and infantry supported by a numerous and powerful artillery: he made several charges with the cavalry upon our infantry, but all were repulsed in the steadiest manner . . .

Although Marshal Blucher had maintained his position at Sambref, he still found himself much weakened by the severity of the contest, in which he had been engaged, and as the fourth corps had not arrived, he determined to fall back, and concentrate his army upon Wavre; and he marched there in the night after the action was over.

This movement of the Marshal's rendered necessary a corresponding one on my part; and I retired from the farm of Quattre Bras upon Genappe, and thence upon Waterloo the next morning, the 17th, at ten o'clock . . .

The position which I took up in front of Waterloo, crossed the high roads from Charleroy and Nivelle, and had its right thrown back to a ravine near Merke Braine, which was occupied: and its left extended to a height above the hamlet of Ter la Haye, which was likewise occupied. In front of the right centre and near the Nivelle road, we occupied the house and garden of Hougoumount, which covered the return of that flank; and in front of the left centre, we occupied the farm of la Haye Sainte. By our left we communicated with Marshal Blucher, at Wavre, through Ohaim; and the marshal had promised me, that in case we should be attacked, he would support me with one or more corps, as might be necessary.

The enemy collected his army, with the exception of the third corps, which had been sent to observe Marshal Blucher, on a range of heights to our front, in the course of the night of the 17th and yesterday morning: and at about ten o'clock he commenced a furious attack upon our post at Hougoumont . . . I am happy to add, that it was maintained throughout the day with the utmost gallantry by these brave troops, notwithstanding the repeated efforts of large bodies of the enemy to obtain possession of it.

This attack upon the right of our centre was accompanied by a very heavy cannonade upon our whole line, which was destined to support the repeated attacks of cavalry and infantry occasionally mixed, but some times separate, which were made upon it. In one of these the enemy carried the farm house of La Haye Sainte, as the detachment of the light battalion of the [King's German] legion which occupied it had expended all its ammunition, and the enemy occupied the only communication there was with them.

The enemy repeatedly charged our infantry with his cavalry, but these attacks were uniformly unsuccessful, and they afforded opportunities to our cavalry to charge, in one of which Lord E. Somerset's brigade, consisting of the life guards, royal horse guards, and 1st dragoon guards, highly distinguished themselves, as did that of Major General Sir W. Ponsonby, having taken many prisoners and an eagle.

These attacks were repeated until about seven in the evening, when the enemy made a desperate effort with the cavalry and infantry, supported by the fire of artillery, to force our left centre near the farm of La Haye Sainte, which after a severe contest was defeated, and having observed that the troops retired from this attack in great confusion, and that the marc[h] of General Bulow's corps by Euschermont upon Planchernerte and la Belle Alliance, had begun to take effect, and as I could perceive the fire of his cannon, and as Marshal Prince Blucher had joined in person, with a corps of his army to the left of our line by Ohaim, I determined to attack the enemy, and immediately advanced the whole line of infantry, supported by the cavalry and artillery. The attack succeeded in every point; the enemy was forced from his position on the heights, and fled in the utmost confusion, leaving behind him, as far as I could judge, one hundred and fifty pieces of cannon, with their ammunition, which fell into our hands. I continued the pursuit till long after dark, and then discontinued it only on account of the fatigue of our troops, and because I found myself on the same road with Marshal Blucher, who assured me of his intention to pursue the enemy throughout the night; he had sent me word this morning that he had taken sixty pieces of cannon belonging to the Imperial Guard, and several carriages, baggage, &c, belonging to Buonaparte, in Genappe . . .

It gives me the greatest satisfaction to assure your Lordship, that the army never, upon any occasion, conducted itself better . . .

I should not do justice to my feelings or to Marshal Blucher and the Prussian army, if I do not attribute the successful result of this arduous day, to the cordial and timely assistance I received from them.

The operation of General Bulow, upon the enemy's flank, was a most decisive one; and even if I had not found myself in a position to make the attack, which produced the final result, it would have forced the enemy to retire, if his attacks should have failed, and would have prevented him from taking advantage of them, if they should unfortunately have succeeded.

I send, with this despatch, two eagles, taken by the troops in action, which Major Percy will have the honour of laying at the feet of his Royal Highness.

I beg leave to recommend him to your Lordship's protection. I have the honour, &c,

WELLINGTON.

NOTES

INTRODUCTION

1 Philip Howes *The Catalytic Wars*
  1998 *passim*
2 Gronow *Reminiscences* 47
3 Tomkinson *Diary* 305
4 Kennedy *Notes* 173

THE CAMPAIGN

1 Bryant *Elegance* 220
2 Fletcher *Desperate* 21
3 *Ibid.*
4 Hibbert *Waterloo* 140–1
5 The revisionist works of Peter
  Hofschröer are important on this
  subject
6 Herold *Waterloo* 67
7 Chandler *Campaigns* 1034–42
8 Fraser *Ball* 11–14
9 *Ibid.* 20–30
10 For an alternative (and much less
  sympathetic) view of
  Wellington's troop movements,
  see Peter Hofschröer's *oeuvre*. For
  a refutation of some of
  Hofschröer's allegations see
  Weller *Wellington* 181–7
11 Fraser *Ball* 3
12 Chandler *Campaigns* 1043
13 Bryant *Elegance* 221
14 O'Neil *Adventures* 228
15 Weller *Waterloo* 183
16 Bryant *Elegance* 223

17 For an explanation of these
  remarks see Roberts *Napoleon*
  passim

THE FIRST PHASE

1 Cotton *Voice* 37
2 Gronow *Reminiscences* 42
3 Cotton *Voice* 37
4 Roberts *Napoleon* 159–60
5 Cotton *Voice* 51
6 Uffindell and Corum *Waterloo* 35
7 Gronow *Reminiscences* 43

THE SECOND PHASE

1 Herold *Waterloo* 124
2 Urban *Rifles* 268–9
3 *Ibid.*
4 Hibbert *Waterloo* 206–7
5 Bryant *Elegance* 224 n2
6 Cotton *Voice* 58
7 Tomkinson *Diary* 303–4

THE THIRD PHASE

1 Keegan *Face* 126
2 Smith *Charge* 233
3 Kennedy *Notes* 115–16
4 Smith *Charge* 117
5 Becke *Waterloo* II 84
6 O'Neil *Adventures* 232
7 Gronow *Reminiscences* 46
8 Becke *Waterloo* II 85

9 Longford *Sword* 568
10 Howarth *Near Run* 143
11 Gronow *Reminiscences* 45
12 *Ibid.* 46
13 Becke *Waterloo* II 98–9
14 Kennedy *Notes* 100
15 Tomkinson *Diary* 308

THE FOURTH PHASE

1 Becke *Waterloo* II 102–3
2 O'Neil *Adventures* 234
3 Howarth *Near Run* 155
4 Urban *Rifles* 272
5 O'Neil *Adventures* 234
6 Kennedy *Notes* 128–9
7 Gronow *Reminiscences* 45

THE FIFTH PHASE

1 Becke *Waterloo* II 114–15
2 Hibbert *Waterloo* 227
3 Fraser *Ball* 50
4 Becke *Waterloo* II 119
5 Gronow *Reminiscences* 47

6 Uffindell and Corum *Waterloo* 41
7 Gronow *Reminiscences* 48
8 Sabine *Letters* 553
9 Cotton *Voice* 138
10 Gronow *Reminiscences* 52

CONCLUSION

1 Ropes *Campaign* 87 and 106, Weller *Waterloo* 183, Fletcher *Desperate* 46–8, Hofschröer *Waterloo passim*
2 Weller *Waterloo* 201
3 *Ibid.* 183–4
4 Roberts *Napoleon passim*
5 Ropes *Campaign* 120–4, Weller *Waterloo* 190–1
6 Becke *Waterloo* I 229
7 *Ibid.* I 44–5, II 20
8 Weller *Waterloo* 194
9 Chesney *Campaign* 192, Weller *Waterloo* 196
10 Cotton *Voice* 138
11 O'Neil *Adventures* 252

CONCISE BIBLIOGRAPHY
AND GUIDE TO FURTHER READING

Adkin, Mark, *The Waterloo Companion: The Complete Guide to History's Most Famous Land Battle* 2001

Becke, A.F., *Napoleon and Waterloo* 2 vols, 1914

Bryant, Arthur, *The Age of Elegance 1812–1822* 1950

Chalfont, Lord (ed.), *Waterloo: Battle of Three Armies* 1979

Chandler, David, *The Campaigns of Napoleon* 1966

Chandler, David, *Waterloo: The Hundred Days* 1981

Chandler, David, *Napoleon's Marshals* 1987

Chandler, David, *On the Napoleonic Wars* 1994

Chesney, Col. Charles, *Waterloo Lectures: A Study of the Campaign of 1815* 1907

Corrigan, Gordon, *Wellington: A Military Life* 2001

Cotton, Edward, *A Voice from Waterloo* 1877

Fletcher, Ian, *Wellington's Regiments: The Men and their Battles from Roliça to Waterloo, 1805–1815* 1996

Fletcher, Ian, *Galloping at Everything: The British Cavalry in the Peninsular War and at Waterloo 1808–15: A Reappraisal* 1999

Fletcher, Ian, *A Desperate Business: Wellington, the British Army and the Waterloo Campaign* 2001

Forrest, Alan, *Napoleon's Men: The Soldiers of the Revolution and Empire* 2002

Fraser, Sir William, *The Waterloo Ball* 1897

Fuller, J.F.C., *The Decisive Battles of the Western World, and their Influence upon History* 1955

Gronow, Captain Howell Rees, *The Reminiscences of Captain Gronow* 1977

Hamilton-Williams, David, *Waterloo: New Perspectives* 1993

Haythornthwaite, Philip, *Waterloo Men: The Experience of Battle 16–18 June 1815* 1999

Herold, J. Christopher, *The Battle of Waterloo* 1967

Hibbert, Christopher, *Waterloo* 1967

Hofschröer, Peter, *1815: The Waterloo Campaign* 1998

Holmes, Richard, *Wellington* 2002

Horsburgh, E.L.S., *Waterloo: A Narrative and a Criticism* 1895

Houssaye, H., *1815* vol. II, 1900

Howarth, David, *A Near Run Thing: The Day of Waterloo* 1968

Jennings, Louis J. (ed.), *The Croker Papers* 3 vols, 1885

Keegan, John, *The Face of Battle* 1976

Kennedy, Sir James Shaw, *Notes on the Battle of Waterloo* 2003

Kincaid, Captain John, *Adventures in the Rifle Brigade* 1830

Longford, Elizabeth, *Wellington: Years of the Sword* 1969

Mercer, Capt. Cavalié, *Journal of the Waterloo Campaign* 1927

Müffling, Baron von, *Passages from my Life* 1853

Muir, Rory, *Britain and the Defeat of Napoleon 1807–1815* 1996

Naylor, J., *Waterloo* 1960

Neillands, Robin, *Wellington and Napoleon: Clash of Arms* 1994

Nofi, Albert, *The Waterloo Campaign, June 1815* 1993

O'Neil, Charles, *The Military Adventures of Charles O'Neil* 1997

Pericoli, Ugo, *1815: The Armies at Waterloo* 1973

Roberts, Andrew, *Napoleon and Wellington* 2001

Ropes, John Codman, *The Campaign of Waterloo: A Military History* 1893

Sabine, Edward (ed.), *Letters of Augustus Frazer* 1859

Saunders, E., *The Hundred Days* 1964

Siborne, Herbert (ed.), *The Waterloo Letters* 1891

Siborne, William, *History of the War in France and Belgium* 2 vols, 1844

Siborne, William, *The Waterloo Campaign* 1904

Smith, Digby, *Charge!: Great Cavalry Charges of the Napoleonic Wars* 2003

Stanhope, Earl, *Notes of Conversations with the Duke of Wellington* 1888

Tomkinson, James (ed.), *The Diary of a Cavalry Officer in the Peninsular War and Waterloo Campaign* 1894

Uffindell, Andrew, *The Eagle's Last Triumph: Napoleon's Victory at Ligny, June 1815* 1994

Uffindell, Andrew and Corum, Michael, *On the Fields of Glory: The Battlefields of the Waterloo Campaign* 1996

Uffindell, Andrew and Corum, Michael, *Waterloo: The Battlefield Guide* 2003

Urban, Mark, *Rifles: Six Years with Wellington's Legendary Sharpshooters* 2003

Weller, Jac, *Wellington at Waterloo* 1967

Weller, Jac, *On Wellington: The Duke and his Art of War* 1998

INDEX